Grandma's Best Recipes

Blueberry Hill

Grandma's Best Recipes

LOVE FOOD™

This edition published in 2013
LOVE FOOD is an imprint of Parragon Books Ltd

Parragon
Chartist House
15–17 Trim Street
Bath, BA1 1HA, UK

www.parragon.com/lovefood

ISBN: 978-1-78186-741-9

Printed in China

Notes for the reader

This book uses both metric and imperial measurements. Follow the same units of measurement throughout; do not mix metric and imperial. All spoon measurements are level: tsp are assumed to be 5 ml, and tbsp are assumed to be 15 ml. Unless otherwise stated, milk is assumed to be full fat, eggs and individual vegetables are medium, and pepper is freshly ground black pepper. Unless otherwise stated, all root vegetables should be washed in plain water and peeled prior to using.

For best results, use a food thermometer when cooking meat and poultry – check the latest government guidelines for current advice.

Garnishes, decorations and serving suggestions are all optional and not necessarily included in the recipe ingredients or method.

The times given are an approximate guide only. Preparation times differ according to the techniques used by different people and the cooking times may also vary from those given. Optional ingredients, variations or serving suggestions have not been included in the time calculations.

Recipes using raw or very lightly cooked eggs should be avoided by infants, the elderly, pregnant women, convalescents and anyone suffering from an illness. Pregnant and breastfeeding women are advised to avoid eating peanuts and peanut products. Sufferers from nut allergies should be aware that some of the ready-made ingredients used in the recipes in this book may contain nuts. Always check the packaging before use.

Contents

Welcome to

Blueberry Hill

The kitchen is the heart of the home, and for many, Grandma is the heart of the kitchen. It was Grandma who created delicious culinary memories for us and we yearn for those scrumptious foods that evoke happy remembrances of home cooking. You'll find those dishes — and those memories — in *Grandma's Best Recipes*.

Whether Grandma came from Ireland in the last century, Italy two generations ago, or France two decades ago, the recipes featured in *Grandma's Best Recipes* express the highest quality of home cooking from a broad range of international origins.

Blueberry Hill Books are produced by a consortium of top-notch cooks and food professionals who have created a collection of hundreds of delectable family-style recipes, from starters to desserts. Each and every dish has been carefully tested, assuring perfect results every time.

Whether you consider yourself a gourmet or a beginner cook, we're sure that our books will soon become a well-used collection on your shelf. In *Grandma's Best Recipes*, you'll find a diverse and delicious range of 130 recipes ranging from Grandma's breakfast dishes through to family meals and sweet treats.

Here's to grandmas everywhere.

Blueberry Hill

Storecupboard Essentials

A well-stocked storecupboard helps to make life a little easier when trying to plan what to cook. The ingredients listed below are the things you'll regularly find on our shopping list.

Dried ingredients

Pasta Spaghetti and macaroni are good basic pastas, but for a broader choice, include lasagne sheets, cannelloni, fusilli, farfalle, tagliatelle and conchiglie.

Rice Every storecupboard should have a good long-grain rice such as basmati rice, supplemented with risotto rice and brown rice.

Noodles Most noodles are associated with south-east Asian cooking. Ensure you have a selection of both egg noodles and rice noodles for use in soups and stir-fries.

Flour Plain flour is great for thickening casseroles, making sauces and coating food before cooking. Self-raising flour is used for baking, while bread-making generally requires specific strong flour due to higher gluten levels.

Sugar Caster sugar, granulated sugar, and muscovado sugar cover the basics, but some recipes will call for icing sugar for making icings and for decoration.

Nuts and seeds Walnuts, almonds, pine kernels and cashews can be used to add extra crunch and texture to savoury dishes and baked goods. Ensure you store them in airtight containers. Sesame seeds are useful for many Asian-inspired dishes.

Oils & vinegars

Extra virgin olive oil Ideal for drizzling over salads, extra virgin olive oil is produced from the first cold-pressing of the olives and is a premium olive oil with a peppery, fruity flavour.

Vegetable oil Made of a blend of various oils, this is best used for frying, as it is very greasy.

Groundnut oil Suitable for drizzling, dressings and mayonnaise as well as use in cooking, this is a very versatile oil.

Wine vinegars Available in many different varieties, mainly red, white and sherry. They can be used for dressings, marinades and sauces, or for drizzling over food.

Balsamic vinegar This delicious vinegar is thick, dark and slightly sweet. It is made from grape juice that is aged in barrels over a number of years.

Herbs & spices

Nothing beats fresh herbs and spices but it's always good to have the following dried herbs and spices to hand.

Chilli powder This powdered mixture of spices includes dried chillies, cumin, coriander and cloves. Use it to flavour soups and stews.

Paprika This spice is made from ground sweet red pepper pods and its flavour can vary from mild, sweet and pungent to fiery hot. It is excellent in salad and as a garnish.

Storecupboard Essentials

Bay leaves Originally from the Mediterranean, dried bay leaves add a good pungent flavour to soups, sauces and casseroles. They are usually discarded once the food has absorbed their flavour.

Thyme A very versatile herb that can be used with meat, poultry, egg and potato dishes and is also good in soups, sauces, roasts, casseroles and stews.

Five spice Chinese five spice seasoning is a blend of cloves, cinnamon, fennel seeds, Szechuan peppercorns and star anise. It is very popular in stir-fries.

Old Bay seasoning Look for this blend of seasonings at speciality shops, or make it by grinding 6 bay leaves, 4 whole cloves, 1 tablespoon each of celery seeds, whole black peppercorns and sweet paprika, ½ teaspoon of whole cardamom seeds and ¼ teaspoon of mace in a spice grinder.

Ginger Dried ginger is particularly good with fruit, biscuits and condiments.

Mixed spice This blend of spices usually consists of cinnamon, cloves, mace, nutmeg, coriander and allspice. It has a warm, sweet flavour and is delicious in fruit desserts, bread, cakes, biscuits, pies and drinks.

Other items

Stock cubes Great for use in casseroles and soups if you do not have time to make or buy fresh stock.

Tomato purée This is a condensed purée, which adds a more intense flavour to sauces and soups.

Canned tomatoes Always useful for a variety of dishes, from sauces and soups to stews and casseroles.

Canned beans Always have a few cans of beans to hand from red kidney beans to lentils and chickpeas. They don't require soaking and can be very useful to have in any storecupboard.

Canned fish Many dishes can use canned or fresh fish. Tuna, crab and anchovies are all useful for salads or pasta dishes.

Pickled foods Pickles, pickled onions and capers make perfect accompaniments and garnishes for meat and vegetable dishes.

Olives It's always useful to have a can or a jar of olives. They are delicious in salads, pastas and on pizzas, or to blend and make dips from.

Soy sauce A popular Chinese sauce, it is used in a lot of south-east Asian dishes and adds a salty flavour. Soy comes in light and dark varieties; use the light one with shellfish and the dark one with duck and meat.

Worcestershire sauce This spicy sauce adds a fantastic fiery flavour to casseroles and soups.

1

Grandma's Breakfast

Eggs Benedict

1 tbsp white wine vinegar

12 fresh large eggs

6 breakfast muffins, halved

12 back bacon rashers

Butter, as needed

For the hollandaise

225 g/8 oz unsalted butter

5 large egg yolks

2 tbsp fresh lemon juice

Cayenne pepper, to taste

Salt, to taste

Sliced fruit, to garnish

Bring a saucepan of lightly salted water with 1 tablespoon of white wine vinegar to a gentle simmer. Working in small batches, poach the eggs, then carefully place them in a bowl of cool water. Reserve until needed.

To make the hollandaise, melt the butter in a small saucepan. In a medium bowl, combine the egg yolks and lemon juice. Place over a saucepan with 5 cm/2 inches of gently simmering water, ensuring the bowl does not touch the water. Whisk constantly until the mixture thickens and is very warm to the touch.

Remove from the heat and slowly drizzle in the melted butter, whisking constantly until it's all incorporated. Season with the cayenne pepper and salt, and whisk. Cover with foil and keep warm until needed.

Bring a large, deep pan filled with 7.5 cm/3 inches of salted water to a simmer. Place the muffin halves on a baking tray and toast under the grill until golden, then brush with butter. Keep in a low, warm oven until needed. Place the bacon rashers on a baking tray and cook under the grill until crispy, turning once. Place one rasher of bacon on each muffin half and return to the warm oven while you reheat the eggs.

Carefully transfer the poached eggs into the simmering water for 2 minutes until just heated through. Remove the eggs with a slotted spoon, and place one on each muffin half. Spoon over the warm hollandaise and serve with sliced fruit.

Spanish Potato Omelette

125 ml/4 fl oz olive oil

450 g/1 lb potatoes, sliced

1 large onion, sliced

1 large garlic clove, crushed

6 large eggs

Salt and black pepper, to taste

Heat the olive oil in a non-stick frying pan over a high heat. Reduce the heat, add the potatoes, onion and garlic and cook for 15–20 minutes, stirring frequently, until the potatoes are tender.

Beat the eggs together in a large bowl and season generously with salt and pepper. Using a slotted spoon, transfer the potatoes and onion to the bowl of eggs. Pour the excess oil from the frying pan into a heatproof jug and reserve, then scrape off the crusty bits from the base of the pan and add to the egg mixture.

Reheat the frying pan over a medium heat. Add about 2 tablespoons of the oil reserved in the jug. Pour in the potato mixture, smoothing the vegetables into an even layer. Cook for about 5 minutes, shaking the frying pan occasionally, or until the base of the omelette is set.

Use a palette knife to loosen the sides of the omelette. Place a large plate face down over the pan. Carefully turn out the omelette onto the plate.

Gently slide the omelette back into the frying pan, cooked side up. Use the palette knife to tuck down the edges. Continue cooking over a medium heat for 3–5 minutes, until set.

Remove the frying pan from the heat and slide the omelette onto a serving plate. Let cool for at least 5 minutes before cutting. Serve hot, warm or at room temperature.

Banana Cinnamon Muffins

makes 12

125 g/4½ oz plain flour

1 tsp baking powder

Pinch of salt

175 g/6 oz golden caster sugar

6 tbsp milk

2 eggs, lightly beaten

175 g/6 oz butter, plus extra for greasing

2 small bananas, mashed

For the icing

55 g/2 oz cream cheese

2 tbsp butter

¼ tsp ground cinnamon

125 g/4½ oz icing sugar

Preheat the oven to 200°C/400°F/Gas Mark 6. Lightly grease a 12-hole muffin tin. Sift together the flour, baking powder and salt into a mixing bowl. Stir in the sugar.

In a separate bowl, whisk the milk, eggs and butter together until combined. Slowly stir into the flour mixture without beating. Fold in the mashed bananas.

Spoon the mixture into the muffin tin and bake in the preheated oven for 20 minutes until risen and golden. Turn out onto a wire rack and leave to cool.

To make the icing, beat the cream cheese and butter together in a bowl until smooth, then beat in the cinnamon and icing sugar until creamy. Chill the icing in the fridge for 15 minutes to firm up, then top each muffin with a dollop of icing and serve.

Potato Pancakes with Smoked Salmon & Dill Crème Fraîche

serves 8

1 kg/2 lb 4 oz potatoes, peeled

½ onion

2 large eggs

3 tbsp plain flour

1 tsp salt

½ tsp black pepper, plus extra to serve

Pinch of cayenne pepper

Vegetable oil, as needed

85–115 g/3–4 oz smoked salmon, thinly sliced

4 tbsp crème fraîche or soured cream

4 tbsp chopped fresh dill

Using a cheese grater, grate the potatoes and quickly transfer to a large bowl of cold water. Grate the onion and add to the bowl. Leave to sit for 20 minutes. To another large mixing bowl, add the eggs, flour, salt, pepper and cayenne, and whisk until smooth. Set aside.

Drain the potato mixture into a colander. Line a baking tray with several layers of kitchen paper. Take a handful of the potato mixture from the colander and squeeze as hard as possible to extract even more water. Place the 'dry' potatoes on the kitchen paper. Spread the potatoes evenly on the baking tray and press down with some more dry kitchen paper. Remove the kitchen paper and tip the potato mixture into the bowl with the egg mixture. Stir to combine thoroughly.

Pour about 5 mm/¼ inch of vegetable oil into a large, heavy-based frying pan (preferably non-stick). Place over a medium–high heat and, when the oil is hot (the surface will begin to shimmer), spoon about a ladleful of the potato mixture into the pan, shape into a round and flatten to about 1 cm/½ inch thick. Reduce the heat to medium and fry the potato pancakes for about 5 minutes on each side or until browned, crispy and cooked through. Drain on kitchen paper and place in a warm oven until you're ready to serve.

To serve, top with the sliced smoked salmon, a dollop of crème fraîche, the fresh dill and a few grinds of pepper.

Corned Beef Hash

2 tbsp butter

1 tbsp vegetable oil

650 g/1 lb 7 oz cooked salt beef, cut in small cubes

1 medium onion, diced

650 g/1 lb 7 oz white potatoes, peeled, cut in small cubes

¼ tsp paprika

¼ tsp garlic powder

Salt and black pepper, to taste

6 poached eggs, to serve

1 tbsp snipped fresh chives, to garnish

Add the butter, oil, salt beef and onion to a large, cold non-stick frying pan. Turn the heat to medium–low and cook, stirring occasionally, while you prepare the potatoes.

Bring a saucepan of salted water to the boil and cook the potatoes for 5–7 minutes (depending on the size), until partially cooked but still quite firm. Drain very well and add to the frying pan with the rest of the ingredients.

Add the paprika and garlic powder and mix together thoroughly with the hot salt beef mixture, pressing down slightly with a palette knife to flatten. Turn up the heat to medium. Every 10 minutes or so, turn the mixture over with a palette knife until it is well-browned on both sides. Take your time – the only real secret to great corned beef hash is to ensure it cooks long enough, so the potatoes are crispy and the cubes of meat nicely caramelised.

Season to taste with salt and pepper. Transfer to plates and top with the poached eggs. Garnish with the chives and serve.

Eggy French Bread

5 large eggs
225 ml/8 fl oz milk
125 ml/4 fl oz single cream
Pinch of salt
1 tbsp sugar
2 tsp vanilla extract
½ tsp cinnamon
Pinch of mixed spice
12 thick slices day-old French bread
85 g/3 oz butter, plus extra for greasing

Preheat the oven to 180°C/350°F/Gas Mark 4. Lightly grease two baking trays and line with foil.

In a large mixing bowl, whisk together the eggs, milk, cream, salt, sugar, vanilla extract, cinnamon and mixed spice. Soak the bread slices in the egg mixture for 20 minutes or until completely saturated.

Melt the butter in a large non-stick frying pan over a medium heat, then lightly brown the slices of bread in batches, for about 2 minutes per side. Don't allow the bread to brown too much as it will continue cooking in the oven.

Transfer the bread to the prepared baking trays and bake for 10 minutes. Remove from the oven and turn each slice over. Return to the oven for a further 10–15 minutes or until browned and the bread springs back slightly when pressed with a finger. Serve immediately.

Lemon Poppy Seed Muffins

makes 16

280 g/10 oz plain flour

½ tsp salt

1½ tsp baking powder

¼ tsp bicarbonate of soda

115 g/4 oz unsalted butter, softened

200 g/7 oz golden caster sugar

Finely grated zest of 2 lemons

2 large eggs

2 tbsp lemon juice

225 ml/8 fl oz soured cream

2 tbsp poppy seeds

For the glaze
1 tbsp lemon juice

3 tbsp icing sugar

Preheat the oven to 180°C/350°F/Gas Mark 4. Line two 12-hole muffin tins with 16 paper muffin cases.

In a mixing bowl, whisk together the flour, salt, baking powder and bicarbonate of soda, and set aside until needed.

In a separate mixing bowl, beat together the butter, sugar and lemon zest until light and creamy. Beat in the eggs one at a time, mixing thoroughly before adding the next. Stir in a third of the flour mixture until just combined. Stir in the lemon juice and half of the soured cream until combined.

Add the remaining flour mixture and stir until combined. Stir in the remaining soured cream and the poppy seeds. Divide the mixture evenly between the muffin cases. Bake in the preheated oven for 30 minutes, or until golden brown and a skewer inserted in the centre comes out clean. While the muffins are baking, mix the lemon juice and icing sugar together to form a thin glaze.

Remove the muffins from the oven when ready and leave to cool for 5 minutes. Brush the lemon glaze evenly over the top of each muffin. When cool enough to handle, remove the muffins from the tins and leave to cool completely on a wire rack before serving.

Baked Spinach & Feta Omelette

serves 6

1 tbsp butter

450 g/1 lb fresh spinach leaves, washed

6 bacon rashers, cut into 5-mm/¼-inch pieces

½ onion, diced

Pinch of cayenne pepper

12 eggs, beaten

150 g/5½ oz feta cheese, crumbled

Salt and black pepper, to taste

Preheat the oven to 180°C/350°F/Gas Mark 4.

Melt the butter in a large saucepan over a high heat, add all the spinach in one go and cover the pan quickly. Leave for 1 minute, uncover and continue cooking, stirring the spinach until just wilted. Transfer to a colander to drain. When the spinach is cool enough to handle, squeeze as much liquid out as possible and chop roughly. Reserve until needed.

Heat a 25–30-cm/10–12-inch ovenproof frying pan over a medium heat and cook the bacon until almost crisp. Add the onion and a pinch of salt, and continue cooking for about 6–7 minutes until the onion is translucent. Any excess bacon fat can be tipped out at this point.

Stir in the spinach. Season with salt, black pepper and cayenne, to taste. When the spinach is heated through, add the eggs and stir to combine thoroughly. Turn off the heat and top with the crumbled feta cheese. Use a knife to press the cheese down into the egg slightly.

Transfer the pan to the preheated oven and bake for 10 minutes, then finish under a medium grill for 3 minutes, or until the eggs are just set and the top is lightly browned. Leave to rest for 5–10 minutes before slicing and serving.

Mexican Eggs

8 large eggs

2 tbsp milk

1 tsp olive oil

1 red pepper, deseeded and thinly sliced

½ fresh red chilli, finely chopped

1 fresh chorizo sausage, casing removed and sliced

4 tbsp chopped fresh coriander

4 slices toasted wholemeal bread, to serve

Pepper, to taste

Beat together the eggs and milk in a large bowl and season to taste with pepper. Set aside.

Heat the oil in a non-stick frying pan over a medium heat, add the red pepper and chilli and cook, stirring frequently, for 5 minutes or until the pepper is soft and starting to brown. Add the chorizo and cook until just browned. Transfer the chorizo mixture to a warmed plate and set aside.

Return the frying pan to the heat, add the egg mixture and cook to a soft scramble. Return the chorizo mixture to the pan, stir to combine and sprinkle over the coriander.

Serve immediately on the toasted bread.

Chocolate Chip Muffins

makes 12

40 g/1½ oz butter, softened, plus extra for greasing

200 g/7 oz golden caster sugar

2 large eggs

150 ml/5 fl oz natural yogurt

5 tbsp milk

250 g/9 oz plain flour

1 tsp bicarbonate of soda

175 g/6 oz plain chocolate chips

Preheat the oven to 200°C/400°F/Gas Mark 6. Lightly grease a 12-hole muffin tin.

Place the butter and sugar in a mixing bowl and beat together with a wooden spoon until light and fluffy. Beat in the eggs, yogurt and milk until thoroughly combined.

Sift the flour and bicarbonate of soda into the mixture and stir until just combined.

Stir in the chocolate chips, then divide the mixture evenly between the muffin holes and bake in the preheated oven for 25 minutes, or until risen and golden.

Remove the muffins from the oven and leave to cool in the tin for 5 minutes. Remove them from the tin and transfer to a wire rack to cool completely.

Sausage & Mushroom Breakfast Frittata

serves 6-8

650 g/1 lb 7 oz potatoes, peeled and cut into 2.5-cm/1-inch chunks

25 g/1 oz butter

175 g/6 oz Cheddar cheese, grated

450 g/1 lb sweet or hot sausages of your choice, casing removed

1 bunch spring onions, chopped

225 g/8 oz button mushrooms, sliced

14 eggs, beaten

4 tbsp milk

1½ tsp salt

½ tsp black pepper

Dash of Tabasco sauce (optional)

Preheat the oven to 150°C/300°F/Gas Mark 2.

Boil the potatoes in salted water until just tender, then drain well. Grease a 33 x 23-cm/13 x 9-inch ovenproof dish with half the butter and add the potatoes. Top with half the cheese.

Brown the sausage meat in a non-stick frying pan over a medium heat, breaking it into small pieces with a wooden spoon as it cooks. When browned, add the spring onions and cook for 2 minutes. Use a slotted spoon to transfer the sausage and onions to the dish.

Pour off any excess fat from the pan and add the remaining butter and mushrooms. Add a pinch of salt and cook, stirring, over a high heat until browned. Transfer the mushrooms to the dish and distribute evenly.

In a mixing bowl, whisk together the eggs, milk, salt, black pepper and Tabasco. Pour over the sausage and mushrooms. Give the dish a shake to ensure the eggs are evenly distributed. Top with the remaining cheese.

Bake for about 35 minutes, or until just set. If liked, place under a hot grill for a minute or two to brown the top. Leave to rest for at least 15 minutes before serving.

Buttermilk Scones

makes 12-14

280 g/10 oz plain flour, plus extra for dusting

2 tsp baking powder

¼ tsp bicarbonate of soda

1 tsp salt

100 g/3½ oz unsalted butter, cut into thin slices, chilled in the freezer

175 ml/6 fl oz cold buttermilk, plus extra for brushing

Preheat the oven to 220°C/425°F/Gas Mark 7 and line a baking tray with greaseproof paper.

In a mixing bowl, whisk together the dry ingredients to thoroughly combine. Cut in the ice-cold butter slices and rub into the mixture using your fingers, until it resembles coarse breadcrumbs.

Make a well in the centre and pour in the cold buttermilk. Stir the dry ingredients into the buttermilk with a fork until a loose, sticky dough is formed. Stop as soon as the mixture comes together. Form into a ball and turn the dough out onto a floured work surface.

With floured hands, pat the dough into a rough rectangle about 20 x 10-cm/8 x 4-inches thick. Fold the dough in thirds (like folding a letter). Repeat this process twice more.

On a lightly floured surface, roll or pat the dough out to about 1-cm/½-inch thick. Use a round biscuit cutter to cut out the scones, and place on the prepared baking tray, a few centimetres apart. You can gather up any extra dough after cutting and repeat to get a few more scones, although the texture may suffer from the extra working.

Make a slight depression in the centre of each scone with your thumb to help them rise evenly. Brush the tops with buttermilk. Bake for 15 minutes, or until risen and golden brown. Cool on a wire rack for 10 minutes before serving.

Cinnamon Swirl Eggy Bread

6 ready-prepared cinnamon swirl buns

4 eggs

225 ml/8 fl oz milk

1 tbsp caster sugar

1 tsp vanilla extract

Pinch of salt

1 tsp ground cinnamon

25 g/1 oz butter

Butter and maple syrup, to serve

Slice the cinnamon swirl buns in half horizontally.

Combine the eggs, milk, sugar, vanilla extract, salt and cinnamon in a large, shallow bowl.

Dip the cinnamon bun slices into the mixture, flipping to coat both sides thoroughly.

Melt the butter in a large non-stick frying pan over a medium heat. Fry the cinnamon bun slices, in batches, for 3–4 minutes on each side until golden and cooked through. Serve immediately with butter and maple syrup.

Blueberry Pancakes

makes 8-10

140 g/5 oz plain flour

2 tbsp granulated sugar

2 tsp baking powder

½ tsp salt

225 ml/8 fl oz buttermilk

40 g/1½ oz butter, melted

1 large egg

140 g/5 oz blueberries, rinsed and patted dry

Vegetable oil, for greasing

Butter and warm maple syrup, to serve

Preheat the oven to 140°C/275°F/Gas Mark 1.

Sift together the flour, sugar, baking powder and salt into a large bowl and make a well in the centre.

In a separate bowl, beat together the buttermilk, butter and egg, then pour the mixture into the well in the dry ingredients. Beat the dry ingredients into the liquid, gradually drawing them in from the sides, until a smooth batter forms. Stir in the blueberries.

Heat a large non-stick frying pan over a medium–high heat until a splash of water dances on the surface. Lightly grease the base of the frying pan with the oil using kitchen paper.

Use a ladle to drop about four tablespoons of the batter into the frying pan and spread it out to a 10-cm/4-inch round. Continue adding as many pancakes as will fit in your frying pan. Leave the pancakes to cook until small bubbles appear on the surface, then flip them over and cook for a further 1–2 minutes until the bases are golden brown.

Transfer the pancakes to a warmed plate and keep warm in the oven while you cook the remaining batter, lightly greasing the frying pan as before. Serve with a knob of butter on top of each pancake and warm maple syrup.

2

Grandma's Soups & Snacks

Sweetcorn & Clam Chowder

serves 4

750 g/1 lb 10 oz live clams or canned clams

2 tbsp dry white wine

55 g/2 oz butter

1 large onion, finely chopped

1 small carrot, finely diced

3 tbsp plain flour

300 ml/10 fl oz fish stock

175 ml/6 fl oz water (only if using canned clams)

450 g/1 lb potatoes, diced

150 g/5½ oz sweetcorn, thawed if frozen

475 ml/16 fl oz milk

Salt and black pepper, to taste

Chopped fresh parsley, to garnish

If using live clams, wash thoroughly under cold running water. Discard any with broken shells or any that refuse to close when tapped. Put the clams into a heavy-based saucepan with the wine. Cover tightly and cook over a medium–high heat for 2–4 minutes, or until they open. Discard any clams that remain closed. Remove the clams from their shells and strain the cooking liquid through a very fine mesh sieve; reserve both.

Melt the butter in a large saucepan over a medium–low heat. Add the onion and carrot and cook for 3–4 minutes, stirring frequently, until the onion is softened. Stir in the flour and continue cooking for 2 minutes.

Slowly add about half the stock and stir well, scraping the base of the pan to mix in the flour. Pour in the remaining stock and the reserved clam cooking liquid or water (if using), and bring to a gentle boil. Stir well.

Add the potatoes, sweetcorn and milk, and stir to combine. Reduce the heat and simmer gently, partially covered, for about 20 minutes, stirring occasionally, until all the vegetables are tender.

Chop the clams, if large. Stir the clams into the chowder and continue cooking for about 5 minutes until heated through. Taste and adjust the seasoning, if needed. Ladle the chowder into bowls and sprinkle with the parsley.

Devilled Eggs

12 large eggs
1 tsp white wine vinegar
4 tbsp mayonnaise
½ tsp Dijon mustard
½ tsp prepared horseradish
¼ tsp Worcestershire sauce
½ tsp salt
Dash of Tabasco sauce
Pinch of cayenne pepper
Paprika or more cayenne pepper, to garnish
1 tbsp thinly sliced chives

Place the eggs in a single layer in a large saucepan and cover with cold water by 2.5 cm / 1 inch. Bring to the boil over a high heat. Turn off the heat, cover tightly with the lid and set a timer for 17 minutes.

Carefully pour off most of the hot water and fill the pan with cold water. Leave to sit for 3 minutes. Pour off most of the water and fill the pan again with cold water. Leave for 15 minutes. Drain and refrigerate the eggs until needed or use straight away.

Peel the eggs under cold running water. Cut the eggs in half lengthways and pop out the yolks into a small mixing bowl, reserving the egg white halves. Add the vinegar, mayonnaise, mustard, horseradish, Worcestershire sauce, salt, Tabasco and cayenne pepper to the egg yolks. Mash and mix with a wire whisk until smooth and light.

Using a spoon, or piping bag with a star nozzle, fill the egg white halves with the yolk mixture. Sprinkle the tops with paprika or cayenne pepper. Chill before serving with the sliced chives.

Hot Spinach & Artichoke Dip

serves 8

2 spring onions, white and light green parts only, chopped

Pinch of salt

25 g/1 oz butter

2 garlic cloves, very finely chopped

300 g/10½ oz frozen chopped spinach, thawed, drained and squeezed dry

400 g/14 oz canned artichoke hearts, drained and roughly chopped

225 g/8 oz soft cheese

4 tbsp crème fraîche or soured cream

¼ tsp Tabasco sauce

Small pinch of nutmeg

55 g/2 oz Parmesan cheese, preferably Parmigiano Reggiano, grated

55 g/2 oz mozzarella cheese, grated

Preheat the oven to 200°C/400°F/Gas Mark 6. Sauté the onions with a pinch of salt in the butter over a medium heat until translucent. Add the garlic, stir to combine and immediately turn off the heat. Set aside.

In a mixing bowl, combine the spinach, artichoke hearts, soft cheese, crème fraîche, Tabasco, nutmeg and Parmesan cheese. Add the onion mixture and stir until thoroughly mixed.

Transfer the mixture to a small ovenproof dish and top with the mozzarella cheese. Bake in the preheated oven for about 25 minutes, or until bubbling and golden. If liked, place under a hot grill for a few minutes to brown the top of the dip.

Deep-fried Chilli Corn Balls

serves 4

6 spring onions, sliced

3 tbsp chopped fresh coriander

150 g/5½ oz canned sweetcorn

1 tsp mild chilli powder

1 tbsp sweet chilli sauce

20 g/¾ oz desiccated coconut

1 egg

50 g/1¾ oz polenta

Oil, for deep-frying

Sweet chilli sauce, to serve

In a large bowl, mix together the spring onions, coriander, sweetcorn, chilli powder, chilli sauce, coconut, egg and polenta until well blended.

Cover the bowl with clingfilm and leave to stand for about 10 minutes.

Heat the oil for deep-frying in a large preheated wok or saucepan to 180°C/350°F, or until a cube of bread browns in 30 seconds.

Carefully drop spoonfuls of the corn mixture into the hot oil. Deep-fry the chilli corn balls, in batches, for 4–5 minutes, or until crispy and deep golden brown.

Remove the chilli corn balls with a slotted spoon, transfer to kitchen paper and leave to drain thoroughly.

Transfer the chilli corn balls to serving plates and serve with sweet chilli sauce, for dipping.

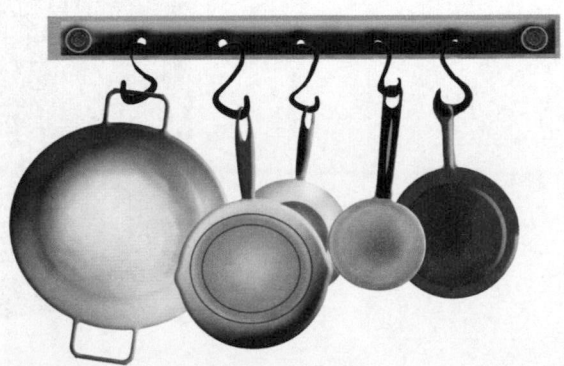

Baked Herb Ricotta

serves 4

1 tbsp olive oil, plus extra for drizzling

1 kg/2 lb 4 oz ricotta cheese, drained

3 eggs, lightly beaten

3 tbsp chopped fresh herbs, such as tarragon, parsley, dill and chives

½ tsp paprika, plus extra for sprinkling

4 slices wholemeal bread

Pepper, to taste

Salad leaves, to serve

Preheat the oven to 180°C/350°F/Gas Mark 4.

Grease a 450-g/1-lb loaf tin with the oil and line with greaseproof paper.

Put the ricotta into a bowl and beat well. Add the eggs and stir until smooth, then stir in the fresh herbs, pepper and paprika.

Spoon the mixture into the prepared tin and put into a roasting tin half-filled with water.

Bake in the preheated oven for 30–40 minutes or until set. Remove from the oven and leave to cool.

Meanwhile, cut the crusts off the bread and toast on both sides. Cut through each slice widthways and cut each slice diagonally into triangles. Arrange in a single layer on a baking tray and bake in the oven for 10 minutes.

Turn out the baked ricotta onto a serving dish, drizzle with a little oil and sprinkle with paprika. Serve with the toast and salad leaves.

Spicy Chicken Wings

makes 30

1.8 kg/4 lb chicken wings
1 tbsp vegetable oil
1 tbsp plain flour
1 tsp salt

For the sauce
150 ml/5 fl oz spicy barbecue sauce
115 g/4 oz cold unsalted butter, cut into 2.5-cm/1-inch slices
1½ tbsp white vinegar
¼ tsp Worcestershire sauce
1 tsp Tabasco sauce
¼ tsp cayenne pepper
Pinch of garlic powder
Salt, to taste

Preheat the oven to 220°C/425°F/Gas Mark 7. If the chicken wings being used were frozen and thawed, make sure they're completely dry before starting the recipe. If using whole wings, cut each into two pieces. The small wing tips can be discarded or saved for stock. In a large mixing bowl, toss the wings with the oil, flour and salt until evenly coated.

Line two heavy-based baking trays with lightly greased foil. Divide the wings and spread out evenly. Do not crowd. Bake in the preheated oven for 25 minutes, remove from the oven and turn the wings over. Return to the oven and cook for a further 20–30 minutes, or until the wings are browned and cooked through. The wings are fully cooked when the bones pull out easily.

While the wings are baking, combine all the sauce ingredients in a saucepan. Bring to a simmer, whisking, over a medium heat. Remove from the heat and reserve. Taste the sauce and adjust the salt and spiciness, if needed.

After the wings are cooked, transfer to a large mixing bowl. Pour the warm sauce over the hot wings and toss with a spoon to completely coat. Serve hot.

Beef Soup with Rice

serves 4

350 g/12 oz lean beef

1 litre/1¾ pints beef stock

1 cinnamon stick, broken in half

2 tbsp dark soy sauce

2 tbsp dry sherry

3 tbsp tomato purée

225 g/8 oz canned water chestnuts, drained and sliced

150 g/5½ oz cooked white rice

1 tsp finely grated orange rind

6 tbsp orange juice

Salt and black pepper, to taste

Strips of orange rind, to garnish

2 tbsp snipped fresh chives, to garnish

Carefully trim away any fat from the beef. Cut into thin strips and place in a large saucepan.

Pour in the stock and add the cinnamon, soy sauce, sherry, tomato purée and water chestnuts. Bring to the boil over a medium heat, skimming off any foam that rises to the surface with a flat ladle or slotted spoon. Cover the pan, reduce the heat to low and simmer gently for 20 minutes, or until the beef strips are tender.

Skim the soup again to remove any more foam. Remove and discard the cinnamon stick and blot the surface of the soup with kitchen paper to remove as much fat as possible.

Stir in the rice, grated orange rind and orange juice. Season to taste with salt and pepper. Heat through for 2–3 minutes before ladling into warmed bowls.

Serve garnished with the strips of orange rind and chives.

Stuffed Tomatoes

serves 4

4 large tomatoes

2 tbsp finely chopped fresh basil

4 tsp olive oil

125 g/4½ oz white mushrooms, very finely chopped

1 small onion, very finely chopped

2 garlic cloves, very finely chopped

1 tbsp chopped fresh parsley

225 ml/8 fl oz vegetable stock

1 tbsp freshly grated Parmesan cheese

Salt and pepper, to taste

Sprigs of fresh basil, to garnish

Preheat the oven to 180°C/350°F/Gas Mark 4.

Slice a lid from the top of each tomato and reserve. Using a teaspoon, carefully scoop out the flesh from the tomatoes and chop. Place the flesh in a bowl and add 1 teaspoon of the basil. Turn over the tomato shells on kitchen paper to drain.

Heat 3 teaspoons of the oil in a non-stick frying pan. Add the mushrooms, onion, garlic, parsley and the remaining basil, and season with pepper to taste. Cover and cook over a low heat for 2 minutes, then remove the lid and cook, stirring occasionally, for a further 8–10 minutes.

Meanwhile, bring the stock to the boil in a pan and cook until reduced by three quarters. Stir in the chopped tomato mixture and cook for a further 3–4 minutes until thickened. Push the mixture through a sieve with a wooden spoon and stir it into the mushroom mixture. Stir in the Parmesan cheese.

Stand the tomatoes in an ovenproof dish and season with salt. Fill each tomato with stuffing and replace the lids. Brush with the remaining oil and bake for 15 minutes, or until tender and cooked through. Serve warm.

Crab Cakes with Tartare Sauce

1 large egg, beaten

2 tbsp mayonnaise

½ tsp Dijon mustard

¼ tsp Worcestershire sauce

½ tsp Old Bay seasoning (see page 11)

¼ tsp salt

Pinch of cayenne pepper

10 cream crackers

450 g/1 lb fresh crabmeat

Plain breadcrumbs

1 tbsp vegetable oil

25 g/1 oz unsalted butter

For the tartare sauce

225 g/8 oz mayonnaise

4 tbsp sweet gherkin relish

1 tbsp very finely chopped onion

1 tbsp chopped capers

1 tbsp chopped parsley

1½ tbsp freshly squeezed lemon juice

Dash of Worcestershire sauce

Few drops of Tabasco sauce

Salt and black pepper, to taste

Whisk together the egg, mayonnaise, mustard, Worcestershire sauce, Old Bay seasoning, salt and cayenne pepper in a mixing bowl. Crush the crackers into very fine crumbs and add to the bowl. Stir until combined and leave to sit for 5 minutes.

Gently fold in the crabmeat. Cover the bowl and refrigerate for at least 1 hour.

Meanwhile, for the sauce, mix together all the ingredients in a bowl. Refrigerate for at least 1 hour before serving.

Sprinkle the breadcrumbs lightly over a large plate. Shape the crab mixture into six cakes and place on the plate. Dust the tops of each crab cake lightly with more breadcrumbs. These cakes are almost all crab, which makes them fragile. They will bind together as the egg cooks and a golden crust forms.

Heat the vegetable oil and butter in a large frying pan over a medium–high heat. When the butter begins to foam, carefully transfer each crab cake to the pan. Sauté for 4 minutes per side until golden brown. Drain on kitchen paper and serve with the tartare sauce, salad leaves and a lemon wedge.

Potato & Spinach Triangles

25 g/1 oz butter, melted, plus extra for greasing

225 g/8 oz new potatoes, finely diced

450 g/1 lb frozen spinach, thawed

1 tomato, deseeded and chopped

¼ tsp chilli powder

½ tsp lemon juice

225 g/8 oz filo pastry, thawed, if frozen

Salt and black pepper, to taste

For the lemon mayonnaise

150 g/5½ oz mayonnaise

2 tsp lemon juice

Zest of 1 lemon

Preheat the oven to 190°C/375°F/Gas Mark 5.

Lightly grease a baking tray with butter.

Bring a pan of lightly salted water to the boil and cook the potatoes for 8–10 minutes, or until cooked through. Drain thoroughly and place in a mixing bowl.

Drain the spinach thoroughly, squeezing out any excess moisture, and add to the potato. Stir in the tomato, chilli powder and lemon juice. Season to taste with salt and pepper.

Lightly brush eight sheets of filo pastry with the melted butter. Spread out four of the sheets and lay the other four on top of them. Cut into 20 x 10-cm/8 x 4-inch rectangles.

Spoon the potato and spinach mixture onto one corner of each rectangle. Fold the corner of the pastry over the filling, then continue folding down the pastry strip in this way to form a triangle.

Place the triangles on the baking tray and bake for 20 minutes, or until golden brown.

To make the lemon mayonnaise, mix together the mayonnaise, lemon juice and lemon zest in a small bowl. Serve the potato and spinach triangles warm or cold with the lemon mayonnaise.

Refried Beans with Tortillas

serves 4

2 tbsp olive oil

1 onion, finely chopped

3 garlic cloves, finely chopped

1 green chilli, chopped

425 g/15 oz canned red kidney beans, drained

425 g/15 oz canned pinto beans, drained

2 tbsp chopped fresh coriander

150 ml/5 fl oz vegetable stock

8 wheat tortillas

55 g/2 oz Cheddar cheese, grated

Salt and pepper, to taste

For the relish

4 spring onions, chopped

1 red onion, chopped

1 green chilli, chopped

1 tbsp garlic-flavoured wine vinegar

1 tsp sugar

1 tomato, chopped

Preheat the oven to 180°C/350°F/Gas Mark 4.

Heat the oil in a large non-stick frying pan. Add the onion and sauté for 3–5 minutes. Add the garlic and chilli and cook for 1 minute.

Mash the beans with a potato masher and stir into the onion mixture with the coriander.

Stir in the stock and cook the beans, stirring, for 5 minutes until soft and pulpy.

Place the tortillas on a baking tray and heat through in the preheated oven for 1–2 minutes.

Mix together the relish ingredients in a small bowl.

Spoon the beans into a serving dish and top with the cheese. Season well. Roll the tortillas and serve with the relish and beans.

Prawn Fritters

serves 4

350 g/12 oz potatoes

3 celery sticks

1 carrot

½ small onion

350 g/12 oz cooked prawns, shelled, thawed if frozen

2½ tbsp plain flour

1 egg, lightly beaten

Vegetable oil, for frying

Salt and black pepper, to taste

For the cherry tomato salsa

12 cherry tomatoes, cut into quarters

½ small mango, finely diced

1 fresh red chilli, deseeded and finely chopped

½ small red onion, finely chopped

1 tbsp chopped fresh coriander

1 tbsp chopped fresh chives

2 tbsp olive oil

2 tsp lemon juice

Salt and black pepper, to taste

For the salsa, mix together all the ingredients in a bowl. Set aside and leave the flavours to infuse while you make the fritters.

Using a food processor or the fine blade of a box grater, finely grate the potatoes, celery, carrot and onion. Combine with the prawns, flour and egg. Season well and set aside.

Divide the prawn mixture into eight equal-sized portions. Press each into a greased 10-cm/4-inch metal pastry cutter (if you have only one cutter, you can simply shape the fritters individually).

Heat a shallow layer of oil in a large frying pan. When hot, transfer the fritters, still in the cutters, to the frying pan, in four batches if necessary. When the oil starts sizzling underneath, remove the cutter.

Cook gently, pressing down with the back of a spoon, for 6–8 minutes on each side, until crisp, browned and the vegetables are tender. Drain on kitchen paper and keep warm while you cook the remaining fritters. Serve hot with the tomato salsa.

Roasted Onion & Pepper Tartlets

serves 4

250 g/9 oz puff pastry, thawed, if frozen

2 red onions

1 red pepper

8 cherry tomatoes, halved

115 g/4 oz mozzarella cheese, shredded

6 sprigs of fresh thyme, chopped

Preheat the grill to medium–high. Preheat the oven to 200°C/400°F/Gas Mark 6.

Roll out the pastry to make 4 x 7.5-cm/3-inch squares. Using a sharp knife, trim the edges of the pastry and reserve the trimmings. Place the pastry squares on a baking tray. Brush a little water along each edge of the pastry squares and use the reserved pastry trimmings to make a rim around each tartlet. Chill the pastry in the refrigerator for 30 minutes.

While the pastry is chilling, prepare the vegetables. Cut the red onions into thin wedges, and halve and deseed the pepper. Place the onions and pepper in a shallow roasting tin. Cook under the preheated grill for 15 minutes, or until the pepper is charred. Place the roasted pepper halves in a polythene bag and allow to sweat for 10 minutes. Peel the skin from the peppers and cut the flesh into strips.

Remove the pastry from the refrigerator and line the inside of the pastry squares with foil. Bake in the preheated oven for 10 minutes. Remove the foil.

Arrange the roasted onions, peppers, tomatoes and cheese evenly among the four tartlets and sprinkle each with fresh thyme. Return the tartlets to the oven and bake for a further 15 minutes, or until the pastry is golden. Serve hot.

Bacon & Lentil Soup

serves 4

450 g/1 lb thick, rindless smoked bacon, diced

1 onion, chopped

2 carrots, sliced

2 celery sticks, chopped

1 turnip, chopped

1 large potato, chopped

100 g/3½ oz green lentils

1 tbsp dried mixed herbs

1 litre/1¾ pints chicken stock or water

Salt and black pepper, to taste

Heat a large, heavy-based saucepan. Add the bacon and cook over a low heat, stirring frequently, for 4–5 minutes until the fat runs. Add the onion, carrots, celery, turnip and potato and cook, stirring frequently, for 5 minutes.

Add the lentils and mixed herbs and pour in the stock. Bring to the boil, then transfer the mixture to a slow cooker. Cover and cook on low for 8–9 hours, or until the lentils are tender.

Season to taste with salt and pepper. Ladle into warmed soup bowls and serve.

Chicken & Sweetcorn Soup

serves 4

175 g/6 oz skinless, boneless chicken breast

2 tbsp vegetable oil

3 spring onions, thinly sliced diagonally

½ large red pepper, thinly sliced

1 garlic clove, crushed

200 g/7 oz baby corn, thinly sliced

1 litre/1¾ pints chicken stock

300 g/10½ oz canned sweetcorn, drained

2 tbsp sherry

3 tsp sweet chilli sauce

3 tsp cornflour

2 tomatoes, cut into quarters, deseeded and sliced

Salt and black pepper, to taste

2 tbsp chopped fresh coriander, to serve

Cut the chicken breast into four strips lengthways, then cut each strip into narrow slices across the grain.

Heat the oil in a wok or large frying pan, swirling it around until it is really hot.

Add the chicken and stir-fry for 3–4 minutes, moving it around the wok until it is well sealed all over and almost cooked through.

Add the spring onions, pepper and garlic, and stir-fry for 2–3 minutes. Add the sliced baby corn and stock, and bring to the boil.

Add the sweetcorn, sherry, sweet chilli sauce and salt to taste, and simmer for 5 minutes, stirring occasionally.

Blend the cornflour with a little cold water. Add to the soup and bring to the boil, stirring until the sauce is thickened. Add the tomato slices, season to taste with salt and pepper and simmer for 1–2 minutes.

Serve hot, sprinkled with the chopped coriander.

Fresh Tomato Tartlets

serves 6

250 g/9 oz ready-made puff pastry, thawed, if frozen

1 egg, beaten

2 tbsp pesto

6 plum tomatoes, sliced

Salt and black pepper, to taste

Fresh thyme leaves, to garnish (optional)

Preheat the oven to 200°C/400°F/Gas Mark 6.

On a lightly floured work surface, roll out the pastry to a 30 x 25-cm/12 x 10-inch rectangle.

Cut the rectangle in half and divide each half into three pieces to make six even-sized rectangles. Chill in the refrigerator for 20 minutes.

Lightly score the edges of the pastry rectangles and brush with the beaten egg.

Divide the pesto evenly between the rectangles and spread out, leaving a 2.5-cm/1-inch border around each.

Arrange the tomato slices in the centre of each rectangle on top of the pesto.

Season well with salt and pepper and lightly sprinkle with fresh thyme leaves, if using.

Bake the tartlets in the preheated oven for 15–20 minutes until well risen and golden brown.

Transfer the tomato tartlets to warmed serving plates and serve while they are still piping hot.

Minestrone Soup

serves 4

2 tbsp olive oil

2 garlic cloves, chopped

2 red onions, chopped

115 g/4 oz prosciutto, sliced

1 red pepper and 1 orange pepper, deseeded and chopped

400 g/14 oz canned chopped tomatoes

1 litre/1¾ pints vegetable stock

1 celery stick, trimmed and sliced

300 g/10½ oz canned borlotti beans, drained

½ small white cabbage, shredded

115 g/4 oz frozen peas, thawed

1 tbsp chopped fresh parsley

115 g/4 oz dried vermicelli

Salt and black pepper, to taste

Freshly grated Parmesan cheese, to garnish

Fresh crusty bread, to serve

Heat the oil in a large saucepan. Add the garlic, onions and prosciutto, and cook over a medium heat, stirring, for 3 minutes until slightly softened.

Add the red and orange peppers and the chopped tomatoes and cook for another 2 minutes, stirring.

Stir in the stock, then add the celery, beans, cabbage, peas and parsley. Season with salt and pepper. Bring to the boil, then lower the heat and simmer for 30 minutes.

Add the vermicelli to the pan. Cook for a further 10–12 minutes, or according to the packet instructions.

Remove from the heat and ladle into serving bowls. Garnish with freshly grated Parmesan cheese and serve with fresh crusty bread.

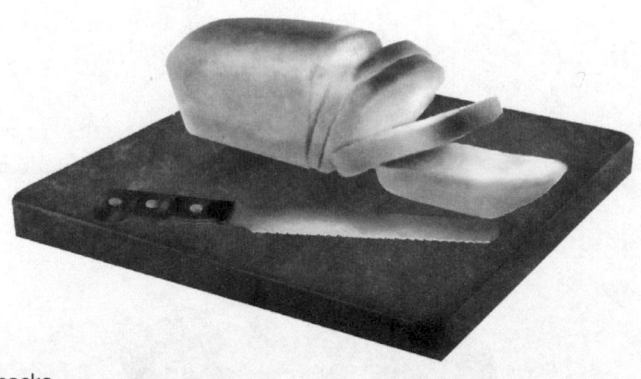

Warm Crab Dip

400 g/14 oz soft cheese

85 g/3 oz Cheddar cheese, grated

225 g/8 oz crème fraîche or soured cream

4 tbsp mayonnaise

2 tbsp lemon juice

2 tsp Dijon mustard

2 tsp Worcestershire sauce, plus extra to taste

500 g/1 lb 2 oz cooked fresh crabmeat

1 garlic clove, halved

Salt and black pepper, to taste

Butter, for greasing

Sprigs of fresh dill, to garnish

Savoury biscuits, to serve

Put the soft cheese into a bowl and stir in the Cheddar cheese, crème fraîche, mayonnaise, lemon juice, mustard and Worcestershire sauce.

Add the crabmeat, season to taste with salt and pepper and gently stir together. Taste and add extra Worcestershire sauce if liked. Cover and leave to chill for 24 hours.

When you are ready to heat the dip, remove it from the refrigerator and let it come to room temperature.

Meanwhile, preheat the oven to 180°C/350°F/Gas Mark 4. Rub the cut sides of the garlic clove over the base and sides of an ovenproof serving dish, then lightly grease.

Spoon the crab mixture into the dish and smooth the surface. Heat the dip through in the preheated oven for 15 minutes. Garnish with fresh dill and serve with savoury biscuits.

Crispy Chicken Goujons with Honey Mustard Dip

serves 8

125 g/4½ oz plain flour

2 tsp salt

1 tsp garlic salt

1 tsp smoked paprika

½ tsp white pepper

4 large skinless, boneless chicken breasts, cut into 1-cm/ ½-inch strips

4 eggs, beaten

1 tbsp milk

300 g/10½ oz Japanese-style panko breadcrumbs

Vegetable oil, for frying

For the dip

115 g/4 oz mayonnaise

2 tbsp Dijon mustard

2 tbsp yellow mustard

1 tbsp rice vinegar

2 tbsp honey

½ tsp hot sauce, optional

Combine the flour, salt, garlic salt, smoked paprika and white pepper in a large, sealable freezer bag. Shake to mix. Add the chicken strips, seal the bag and shake vigorously to coat evenly.

In a mixing bowl, whisk together the eggs and milk. Add the chicken strips, shaking off the excess flour as you remove them from the bag. Stir until the strips are completely coated in the egg mixture.

Pour the breadcrumbs into a shallow pan. Use one hand to remove the chicken strips from the egg mixture, a few at a time, allowing the excess egg to drip off, and place in the pan of breadcrumbs. Use the other hand to coat the chicken in the breadcrumbs, pressing them in firmly. Place the strips on baking trays or racks while you complete the remaining strips. When finished, allow the chicken strips to rest for 10–15 minutes before frying.

Pour about 1 cm/½ inch of oil into a large, heavy-based frying pan set over a medium–high heat. Heat the oil until it reaches 180–190°C/350–375°F or a small cube of bread browns in 30 seconds. Cook the chicken strips for 2–3 minutes per side, or until golden brown and cooked through. Work in batches, drain on kitchen paper and keep the cooked chicken goujons warm in a warm oven.

To make the honey mustard dip, combine all the ingredients in a bowl and mix well. Serve immediately.

Tuna-stuffed Tomatoes

4 large tomatoes

2 tbsp sun-dried tomato purée

2 egg yolks

2 tsp lemon juice

Finely grated rind of 1 lemon

4 tbsp olive oil

140 g/5 oz canned tuna, drained

2 tbsp capers, rinsed

Salt and black pepper, to taste

2 sun-dried tomatoes, cut into strips

Fresh basil leaves, to garnish

Preheat the oven to 200°C/400°F/Gas Mark 6.

Halve the tomatoes, scoop out the flesh and discard. Divide the sun-dried tomato purée among the tomato halves and spread around the inside of the skin.

Place on a baking tray and roast in the preheated oven for 12–15 minutes. Leave to cool slightly.

In a food processor, blend the egg yolks and lemon juice with the lemon rind until smooth. Once mixed and, with the motor still running slowly, gradually add the olive oil in a steady stream. Stop the processor as soon as the mayonnaise has thickened. Alternatively, use a hand whisk, beating the mixture constantly until it thickens.

Add the tuna and capers to the mayonnaise and season to taste with salt and pepper.

Spoon the tuna mayonnaise mixture into the tomato shells and garnish with the sun-dried tomato strips and basil leaves. Return the stuffed tomatoes to the oven for a few minutes to heat through, or serve chilled.

Vegetable Soup with Cannellini Beans

serves 4

1 small aubergine

2 large tomatoes

1 potato

1 carrot

1 leek

400 g/14 oz canned cannellini beans

1 litre/1¾ pints hot vegetable or chicken stock

2 tsp dried basil

55 g/2 oz dried ceps, soaked for 10 minutes in enough warm water to cover

85 g/3 oz vermicelli

3 tbsp pesto

Freshly grated Parmesan cheese, to serve (optional)

Slice the aubergine into rings about 1 cm/½ inch thick, then cut each ring into four pieces. Cut the tomatoes and potato into small dice. Cut the carrot into sticks, about 2.5 cm/1 inch long, and cut the leek into rings.

Place the cannellini beans and their liquid in a large pan. Stir in the aubergine, tomatoes, potatoes, carrot and leek.

Add the stock to the pan and bring to the boil. Reduce the heat and allow to simmer for 15 minutes.

Add the basil, dried mushrooms and their soaking liquid and the vermicelli, and simmer for 5 minutes or until the vegetables are tender.

Remove the pan from the heat and stir in the pesto.

Serve with the freshly grated Parmesan cheese, if using.

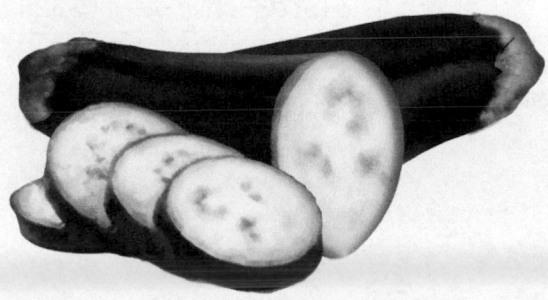

Clam Chowder

225 ml/8 fl oz water

450 g/1 lb live clams, washed

1 tbsp butter

2 bacon rashers, cut into 5-mm/¼-inch pieces

½ onion, diced

2 tbsp flour

450 ml/16 fl oz cold clam liquor (part of this may be made up from the drained canned clam liquid, but fresh clam cooking liquor is stronger)

650 g/1 lb 7 oz potatoes, cut into 5-mm/¼-inch cubes

550 g/1 lb 4 oz canned whole clams, drained

225 ml/8 fl oz milk

225 ml/8 fl oz single cream

Salt and black pepper, to taste

Freshly chopped parsley, to garnish

Savoury biscuits, to garnish

Bring the water to the boil in a small saucepan over a high heat. Discard any clams with broken shells or any that refuse to close when tapped. Add the live clams, cover tightly and cook for 1–2 minutes until the clams open. Transfer to a bowl and reserve. Discard any clams that remain closed. Strain the cooking liquor and allow to cool.

Heat the butter in a large saucepan over a medium heat and cook the bacon until almost crisp. Remove with a slotted spoon and reserve, leaving the butter and bacon fat in the pan.

Reduce the heat to medium–low and add the onion. Sauté for about 5 minutes until soft and translucent. Add the flour and cook, stirring, for 2 minutes. Whisk in the cold clam liquor, slowly at first. Bring back to a simmer and add the potatoes. Cover and cook for 20 minutes or until the potatoes are tender. At this point you can smash some of the potatoes against the base of the pan with a vegetable masher to add body to the soup, if liked.

Stir in the canned clams, milk and cream. Reduce the heat to low and cook until just heated through, but do not boil. Add the reserved clams and cook for a further minute. Season to taste with salt and black pepper.

Serve piping hot topped with the reserved bacon, chopped parsley and savoury biscuits.

Potato Skins with Guacamole

serves 4

4 x 225 g/8 oz baking potatoes

2 tsp olive oil

Coarse sea salt and black pepper, to taste

Snipped fresh chives, to garnish

For the guacamole

225 g/8 oz ripe avocado, mashed

1 tbsp lemon juice

2 ripe, firm tomatoes, finely chopped

1 tsp grated lemon rind

115 g/4 oz low-fat soft cheese with herbs and garlic

4 spring onions, finely chopped

Few drops of Tabasco sauce

Salt and black pepper, to taste

Preheat the oven to 200°C/400°F/Gas Mark 6. Bake the potatoes in the preheated oven for 1¼ hours. Remove from the oven and leave to cool for 30 minutes. Increase the oven temperature to 220°C/425°F/Gas Mark 7.

Halve the potatoes lengthways and scoop out 2 tablespoons of the flesh from each and discard.

Slice in half again. Place on a baking tray and lightly brush the flesh side with oil. Sprinkle with the sea salt and pepper to taste. Bake for a further 25 minutes until golden and crisp.

To make the guacamole dip, mash the avocado with the lemon juice. Add the remaining ingredients and mix.

Once cooked, drain the potato skins on kitchen paper and transfer to a warm serving platter. Garnish with the chives. Pile the guacamole into a serving bowl and serve alongside the potato skins.

Stuffed Mushrooms

serves 4

8 field mushrooms

1 tbsp olive oil

1 small leek, chopped

1 celery stick, chopped

115 g/4 oz firm tofu, diced

1 courgette, chopped

1 carrot, chopped

70 g/2½ oz dried wholemeal breadcrumbs

2 tbsp chopped fresh basil

1 tbsp tomato purée

2 tbsp pine kernels

85 g/3 oz Cheddar cheese, grated

150 ml/5 fl oz vegetable stock

Salt and black pepper, to taste

Preheat the oven to 220°C/425°F/Gas Mark 7. Remove the stalks from the mushrooms and chop them finely. Reserve the caps.

Heat the olive oil in a large heavy-based frying pan over a medium heat. Add the mushroom stalks, leek, celery, tofu, courgette and carrot and cook, stirring constantly, for 3–4 minutes.

Stir in the breadcrumbs, basil, tomato purée and pine kernels. Season with salt and pepper to taste and mix thoroughly. Divide the stuffing mixture evenly between the mushroom caps and sprinkle with the grated cheese. Arrange the mushrooms in a shallow ovenproof dish and carefully pour the stock around them.

Cook in the oven for 20 minutes or until the mushrooms are cooked through and the cheese has melted and browned. Remove the mushrooms from the dish and serve.

Chicken & Pasta Broth

serves 6

For the stock

1 x 1.8–2.25 kg/4–5 lb whole chicken

1 carrot, chopped

1 celery stick, chopped

1 onion, chopped

1 garlic clove

4 sprigs thyme

1 bay leaf

1 whole clove

1 tsp tomato ketchup

Salt and black pepper, to taste

For the soup

1 tbsp butter

1 onion, diced

2 large carrots, diced

2 celery sticks, diced

¼ tsp poultry seasoning

200 g/7 oz dried pasta shapes

1 tbsp chopped parsley

Salt and black pepper, to taste

Preheat the oven to 230°C/450°F/Gas Mark 8. Season the chicken inside and out with salt and pepper. Add the carrot, celery and onion to an oiled 33 x 23-cm/13 x 9-inch roasting tin and place the chicken on top. Roast for 1 hour or until the chicken is tender and the juices run clear when a skewer is inserted into the thickest part of the meat. Remove the chicken from the oven and allow to rest until cool enough to handle. Pull off the breast, thigh and leg meat, and refrigerate until needed.

Transfer the chicken carcass and vegetables from the roasting tin to a large pot. Add 2 litres/3½ pints of cold water, the garlic, thyme, bay leaf, clove and ketchup. Bring to the boil, turn the heat down to low, and simmer for 2 hours. Top the pot up with water as needed to maintain the level of liquid.

While the stock is simmering, place a large saucepan over a medium–low heat. Melt the butter and sauté the diced onion, carrots and celery for 15 minutes, until they begin to soften. Stir in the poultry seasoning, turn off the heat and reserve until the stock is finished cooking.

Skim the fat from the stock and strain into the saucepan with the sautéed vegetables. Bring to the boil, turn the heat to low and simmer until the vegetables are tender. Season to taste with salt and pepper. Turn the heat up to high, add the pasta and boil for 7 minutes. Dice the roast chicken and add to the pan. Turn the heat to medium and simmer until the pasta is tender. Stir in the parsley and serve piping hot.

Vegetable Cake

serves 4-6

For the base

2 tbsp vegetable oil, plus extra for brushing

1.25 kg/2 lb 12 oz waxy potatoes, sliced

For the topping

1 tbsp vegetable oil

1 leek, chopped

1 courgette, grated

1 red pepper, deseeded and diced

1 green pepper, deseeded and diced

1 carrot, grated

2 tsp chopped fresh parsley

225 g/8 oz soft cheese

55 g/2 oz mature Cheddar cheese, grated

2 eggs, beaten

Salt and black pepper, to taste

Shredded cooked leek, to garnish

Salad, to serve

Preheat the oven to 190°C/375°F/Gas Mark 5.

Brush a 20-cm/8-inch springform cake tin with oil.

To make the base, heat the oil in a large non-stick frying pan. Cook the potato slices until softened and browned. Drain on kitchen paper and place in the base of the prepared cake tin.

To make the topping, heat the oil in a separate frying pan. Add the leek and cook over a low heat, stirring frequently, for 3–4 minutes until softened. Add the courgette, peppers, carrot and parsley to the frying pan and cook over a low heat for 5–7 minutes or until the vegetables have softened.

Meanwhile, beat the cheeses and eggs together in a bowl. Stir in the cooked vegetables and season to taste with salt and pepper. Spoon the mixture evenly over the potato base and press down lightly. Transfer to the preheated oven and cook for 20–25 minutes until the cake is set.

Remove the vegetable cake from the tin and transfer to a warmed serving plate. Garnish with the shredded leek and serve with a crisp salad.

Crab Cakes with Salsa Verde

serves 4-6

400 g/14 oz crabmeat

5 x 250 g/9 oz white fish fillet, such as sea bass, cod or plaice, skinned and chopped

1 fresh red chilli, deseeded and chopped

1 garlic clove, chopped

2.5-cm/1-inch piece of fresh ginger, chopped

1 lemon grass stalk, chopped

3 tbsp chopped fresh coriander

1 egg white

2 tbsp vegetable oil, for frying

For the salsa verde

2 fresh green chillies, deseeded and chopped

8 spring onions, chopped

2 garlic cloves, chopped

1 bunch of fresh parsley

Grated rind and juice of 1 lime

Juice of 1 lemon

4 tbsp olive oil

1 tbsp green Tabasco sauce

Salt and black pepper, to taste

Place the crabmeat, fish, red chilli, garlic, ginger, lemon grass, coriander and egg white in a food processor and process until thoroughly blended, then transfer to a bowl, cover with clingfilm and leave to chill in the refrigerator for 30–60 minutes.

Meanwhile, make the salsa verde. Put the green chillies, spring onions, garlic and parsley in a food processor and process until finely chopped. Transfer to a small bowl and stir in the lime rind, lime and lemon juice, olive oil and green Tabasco. Season to taste with salt and pepper, cover with clingfilm, and chill in the refrigerator until ready to serve.

Heat the vegetable oil in a non-stick frying pan. Add spoonfuls of the crab mixture spaced well apart, then flatten gently with a spatula. Cook for 4 minutes then turn over and cook the other side for 3 minutes, or until golden brown. Remove from the frying pan and keep warm while you cook the remaining crab cakes, adding more oil if necessary. Transfer the crab cakes to a large serving plate and serve with the salsa verde.

Prawn Cocktail

900 g/2 lb jumbo prawns deveined, but unpeeled

1 lemon, cut into wedges, to serve

For the cocktail sauce

140 g/5 oz tomato ketchup

4 tbsp chilli sauce

4 tbsp horseradish, or to taste

1 tsp fresh lemon juice

1 tsp Worcestershire sauce

Dash of hot sauce (optional)

Pinch of salt

For the poaching liquid

3 litres/5¼ pints cold water

½ onion, sliced

2 garlic cloves, bruised

2 sprigs tarragon

1 bay leaf

1 tbsp Old Bay seasoning (see page 11)

Juice of ½ lemon

1 tsp black peppercorns

Look for frozen prawns that are deveined (meaning the intestinal tract has been removed), but with the shell on. These prawns make the best prawn cocktail as the shells add flavour when they are poached. If you can't find this type, get shell-on prawns.

For the sauce, combine all the ingredients in a small bowl, mix thoroughly and refrigerate for at least 1 hour before serving.

If you have shell-on prawns use a pair of scissors to make a cut through each shell, down the back of the prawn. Then use a small sharp knife to make a 3-mm/⅛-inch deep incision and remove the intestinal tract. Rinse under cold water.

Add all the poaching liquid ingredients to a large saucepan. Place over a high heat and bring to a simmer. Turn the heat down to low and simmer for 30 minutes.

Fill a mixing bowl with iced water and set aside. Turn up the heat for the poaching liquid to high and bring to the boil. Add the prawns and boil for 5 minutes, or until cooked through. Transfer the prawns to the iced water.

When the prawns are cold, drain well and serve either as they are or shelled with the cocktail sauce and lemon wedges.

Chicken, Bacon & Avocado Salad

serves 4

1 tbsp olive oil

8 bacon rashers

4 large handfuls mixed baby salad leaves, torn into bite-sized pieces

3 hard-boiled eggs, peeled and chopped

450 g/1 lb cooked chicken, cubed

2 avocados, peeled, pitted and cubed

150 g/5½ oz cherry tomatoes, halved

85 g/3 oz Roquefort cheese, crumbled

½ tsp Dijon mustard

4 tbsp red wine vinegar

1 tsp Worcestershire sauce

1 garlic clove, crushed into a paste

¼ tsp salt

¼ tsp black pepper

5 tbsp olive oil

Heat the oil in a large non-stick frying pan over a medium heat and cook the bacon until crisp, then drain on kitchen paper. When cool enough to handle, crumble the bacon and set aside.

Arrange beds of salad leaves in four shallow bowls. Divide the eggs, bacon, chicken, avocados, tomatoes and Roquefort cheese between the bowls and place in rows on top of the salad leaves, covering the surface completely.

In a bowl, whisk together the mustard, vinegar, Worcestershire sauce, garlic, salt and pepper.

Slowly drizzle in the olive oil, whisking constantly, to form a dressing.

Drizzle the dressing evenly over the salads and serve immediately.

Tomato & Cheese Bruschettas

serves 4

8 slices farmhouse-style bread

4 garlic cloves, crushed

25 g/1 oz butter

1 tbsp chopped basil

4 large, ripe tomatoes

1 tbsp tomato purée

8 black olives, stoned and halved

40 g/1½ oz mozzarella cheese, sliced

Salt and black pepper, to taste

Fresh basil leaves, to garnish

For the dressing

1 tbsp extra virgin olive oil

2 tsp lemon juice

1 tsp clear honey

Toast the slices of bread under a hot grill for 2–3 minutes until golden.

Beat the garlic, butter and basil together and spread evenly on each slice.

Cut a cross shape at the top of each tomato. Plunge the tomatoes into a bowl of boiling water – this will make the skin easier to peel. After a few minutes pick each tomato up with a fork and peel off the skin. Chop the tomato flesh and mix with the tomato purée and olives. Divide the mixture between the slices of toast.

Mix the dressing ingredients in a separate bowl and drizzle over the toast. Arrange the mozzarella on top and season to taste with salt and pepper.

Return the toast to the grill for 1–2 minutes until the cheese has melted. Serve garnished with the basil leaves.

Pork & Vegetable Soup

1 tbsp vegetable oil or chilli oil

1 garlic clove, chopped

3 spring onions, trimmed and sliced

1 red pepper, deseeded and finely sliced

2 tbsp cornflour

1 litre/1¾ pints vegetable stock

1 tbsp soy sauce

2 tbsp rice wine or dry sherry

175 g/6 oz pork fillet, finely sliced

1 tbsp finely chopped lemon grass

1 small red chilli, deseeded and finely chopped

1 tbsp grated fresh ginger

115 g/4 oz fine egg noodles

90 g/3¼ oz canned water chestnuts, drained and sliced

Salt and black pepper, to taste

Heat the oil in a large saucepan. Add the garlic and spring onions and cook over a medium heat, stirring, for 3 minutes until slightly softened. Add the pepper and cook, stirring, for a further 5 minutes.

In a bowl, mix the cornflour with enough of the stock to make a smooth paste and stir it into the pan. Cook, stirring constantly, for 2 minutes. Stir in the remaining stock, the soy sauce and rice wine, then add the pork, lemon grass, chilli and ginger. Season with salt and pepper to taste. Bring to the boil, then lower the heat and simmer for 25 minutes.

Fill a separate pan with water and bring the water to the boil. Add the noodles and cook for 3 minutes, or according to the packet instructions. Remove from the heat, drain, then add the noodles to the soup along with the water chestnuts. Cook for a further 2 minutes, then remove from the heat and ladle into serving bowls. Serve immediately.

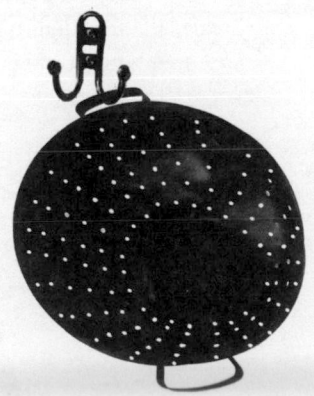

Jacket Potatoes with Beans

serves 6

1.8 kg/4 lb baking potatoes

2 tbsp vegetable oil

1 large onion, chopped

2 garlic cloves, crushed

1 tsp ground turmeric

1 tbsp cumin seeds

2 tbsp mild curry paste

400 g/14 oz canned chopped tomatoes

425 g/15 oz canned black-eyed beans, drained and rinsed

425 g/15 oz canned red kidney beans, drained and rinsed

1 tbsp lemon juice

2 tbsp tomato purée

150 ml/5 fl oz water

2 tbsp chopped fresh mint or coriander

Salt and black pepper, to taste

Preheat the oven to 180°C/350°F/Gas Mark 4.

Scrub the potatoes and prick several times with a fork. Place in a roasting tin and cook for 1–1¼ hours, or until the potatoes feel soft when gently squeezed.

About 20 minutes before the end of cooking time, prepare the topping. Heat the oil in a large frying pan over a medium heat, then add the onion, reduce the heat to low and cook, stirring frequently, for 5 minutes. Add the garlic, turmeric, cumin seeds and curry paste, and cook gently for a further minute.

Stir in the tomatoes, black-eyed beans, red kidney beans, lemon juice, tomato purée, water and chopped mint. Season to taste with salt and pepper, then cover and simmer over a low heat, stirring frequently, for 10 minutes.

When the potatoes are cooked, cut them in half and mash the flesh lightly with a fork. Spoon the prepared bean mixture on top. Place on warmed serving plates and serve immediately.

Niçoise Pasta Salad

serves 4

350 g/12 oz dried conchiglie

115 g/4 oz green beans

55 g/2 oz canned anchovy fillets, drained

2 tbsp milk

2 small heads of crisp lettuce, such as cos

3 large tomatoes

4 hard-boiled eggs

140 g/5 oz canned tuna in oil, drained

100 g/3½ oz black olives, stoned

Salt, to taste

For the vinaigrette

4 tbsp extra virgin olive oil

2 tbsp white wine vinegar

1 tsp wholegrain mustard

Salt and black pepper, to taste

To make the vinaigrette, beat together the oil, vinegar and mustard in a bowl. Season to taste with salt and pepper and refrigerate until ready to serve.

Bring a large saucepan of lightly salted water to the boil over a medium heat. Add the pasta and cook for 8–10 minutes, or according to the packet instructions, until tender but still firm to the bite. Drain the pasta thoroughly and refresh in cold water.

Bring a small saucepan of lightly salted water to the boil over a medium heat. Add the green beans and cook for 5 minutes, or until done. Drain thoroughly and refresh in cold water, then drain again and set aside.

Put the anchovies in a shallow bowl, then pour over the milk and set aside for 10 minutes. Meanwhile, tear the lettuce into large pieces. Score a cross in the tops of the tomatoes and blanch in boiling water for 1–2 minutes, then drain. Skin and roughly chop the flesh. Shell the eggs and cut into quarters. Flake the tuna into large chunks.

Drain the anchovies and the pasta. Put all the salad ingredients into a large bowl, gently mix together and season to taste with salt. Just before serving, pour the vinaigrette over the salad.

Turkey & Lentil Soup

serves 4

1 tbsp olive oil

1 garlic clove, chopped

1 large onion, chopped

300 g/10½ oz mushrooms, sliced

1 red pepper, deseeded and chopped

6 tomatoes, skinned, deseeded and chopped

1 litre/1¾ pints chicken stock

150 ml/5 fl oz red wine

100 g/3½ oz cauliflower florets

1 carrot, chopped

200 g/7 oz red lentils

850 g/1 lb 14 oz cooked turkey, chopped

1 courgette, chopped

Salt and black pepper, to taste

1 tbsp shredded fresh basil, plus extra leaves, to garnish

Heat the oil in a large saucepan over a medium heat. Add the garlic and onion and cook, stirring, for 3 minutes until slightly softened. Add the mushrooms, pepper and tomatoes and cook, stirring, for a further 5 minutes.

Pour in the stock and red wine, then add the cauliflower, carrot and red lentils. Season to taste with salt and pepper.

Bring to the boil, then lower the heat and simmer for 25 minutes until the vegetables are tender and cooked through.

Add the turkey and courgette to the pan and cook for 10 minutes. Stir in the shredded basil and cook for a further 5 minutes, then remove from the heat and ladle into serving bowls. Garnish with fresh basil and serve immediately.

Rösti with Tomato Sauce

450 g/1 lb waxy potatoes

1 carrot, finely diced

1 celery stick, finely diced

55 g/2 oz white mushrooms, diced

1 onion, diced

2 garlic cloves, crushed

55 g/2 oz frozen peas, thawed

85 g/3 oz Parmesan cheese, freshly grated

4 tbsp vegetable oil

25 g/1 oz butter

Salt and black pepper, to taste

For the sauce

325 g/11½ oz passata

2 tbsp chopped fresh coriander

1 tbsp soy sauce

½ tsp chilli powder

2 tsp muscovado sugar

2 tsp mild mustard

5 tbsp vegetable stock

Bring a saucepan of lightly salted water to the boil, add the potatoes and boil for 10 minutes. Drain and set aside to cool. Meanwhile, bring another saucepan of lightly salted water to the boil and cook the carrot for 5 minutes.

When the potatoes are cool enough to handle, grate them with a coarse grater.

Drain the carrot and add it to the grated potatoes with the celery, mushrooms, onion, garlic, peas and cheese. Season to taste with salt and pepper.

Combine all of the sauce ingredients in a small saucepan and bring to the boil. Reduce the heat to low and simmer for 15 minutes.

Divide the potato mixture into 8 equal-sized portions and shape into flattened rectangles with your hands.

Heat the oil and butter in a large non-stick frying pan over a medium heat. Reduce the heat to low and cook the rösti in batches for 4—5 minutes on each side, or until crisp and golden brown. Transfer the rösti to a warmed serving plate and serve immediately with the tomato sauce.

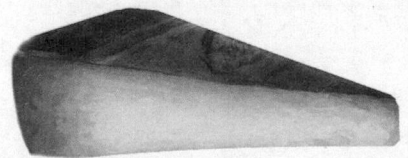

Sweet Potato Patties

serves 6

500 g/1 lb 2 oz sweet potato

2 garlic cloves, crushed

1 small fresh green chilli, chopped

2 sprigs of fresh coriander, chopped

1 tbsp dark soy sauce

Plain flour, for shaping

Vegetable oil, for frying

Sesame seeds, for sprinkling

For the soy-tomato sauce

2 tsp vegetable oil

1 garlic clove, finely chopped

1½ tsp finely chopped fresh ginger

3 tomatoes, skinned and chopped

2 tbsp dark soy sauce

1 tbsp lime juice

2 tbsp chopped fresh coriander

To make the soy-tomato sauce, heat the oil in a wok and stir-fry the garlic and ginger for about 1 minute. Add the tomatoes and stir-fry for a further 2 minutes. Remove from the heat and stir in the soy sauce, lime juice and chopped coriander. Set aside and keep warm.

Finely grate the sweet potatoes (you can do this with a food processor). Place the garlic, chilli and coriander in a mortar and crush to a smooth paste with a pestle. Stir in the soy sauce and mix with the sweet potatoes.

Divide the mixture into 12 equal-sized portions. Dip into the flour and pat into a flat, round patty shape, shaking off any excess.

Heat a shallow layer of oil in a wide frying pan. Cook the sweet potato patties in batches over a high heat until golden, turning once.

Drain on kitchen paper and sprinkle with the sesame seeds. Serve hot, with a spoonful of the soy-tomato sauce.

3

Grandma's Family Meals

Whole Roast Garlic & Herb Chicken with Gravy

4 garlic cloves

5 tbsp olive oil

2 tsp very finely chopped fresh thyme leaves

2 tsp very finely chopped fresh rosemary

1 tsp dried Italian herbs

1 x 2.25-kg/5-lb whole chicken, rinsed and dried with kitchen paper

Salt and black pepper, to taste

For the gravy

1½ tbsp reserved chicken fat

1 tbsp butter

1 heaped tbsp flour

475 ml/16 fl oz cold chicken stock

½ tsp balsamic vinegar

4 sprigs fresh thyme

Salt and black pepper, to taste

Preheat the oven to 230°C/450°F/Gas Mark 8.

Peel the garlic cloves and crush with the flat edge of a knife. Chop very finely and press to a very fine paste.

Combine the olive oil, garlic, thyme, rosemary and dried herbs in a large mixing bowl. Rub the chicken inside and out with the mixture. Continue or leave to marinade in the refrigerator overnight or for a few hours.

Place the chicken in a large roasting tray. Season the cavity with salt and black pepper. Truss the legs with kitchen string.

Place in the centre of the preheated oven and roast for 1 hour or until the chicken is tender and the juices run clear when a skewer is inserted into the thickest part of the meat. Remove the chicken, place on a platter and cover with foil. Leave to rest while making the gravy.

Pour off the excess chicken fat from the tray, reserving 1½ tablespoons. Place the tray back on the hob and add the butter. Once the butter has melted add a little flour and cook, stirring constantly with a whisk, until golden brown. Whisk the cold chicken stock, balsamic vinegar and thyme. Turn the heat to high and boil for 5 minutes, stirring, until the gravy has thickened.

Grandma's Meatloaf

serves 6-8

3 garlic cloves, peeled

1 large carrot, diced

1 celery stick, diced

1 onion, diced

1 red pepper, deseeded and diced

4 large white mushrooms, sliced

25 g/1 oz butter

1 tbsp olive oil

1 tsp dried thyme

2 tsp finely chopped fresh rosemary

1 tsp Worcestershire sauce

4 tbsp tomato ketchup

½ tsp cayenne pepper

1 kg/2 lb 4 oz lean steak mince

2 tsp salt

1 tsp black pepper

2 eggs, beaten

100 g/3½ oz dried breadcrumbs

For the glaze

2 tbsp muscovado sugar

2 tbsp tomato ketchup

1 tbsp Dijon mustard

Pinch of salt

Preheat the oven to 160°C/325°F/Gas Mark 3. Lightly grease a shallow roasting tin. Add the garlic, carrot, celery, onion, red pepper and white mushrooms to a food processor. Pulse on and off until the vegetables are very finely chopped.

Add the butter and olive oil to a large frying pan over a medium heat. When the butter melts, add the vegetable mixture and cook, stirring, for 10 minutes.

Remove from the heat and stir in the thyme, rosemary, Worcestershire sauce, ketchup and cayenne pepper. Set aside and leave to cool to room temperature.

Place the steak mince in a large mixing bowl. Very gently break up the meat with your fingers. Add the cooled vegetable mixture, salt, black pepper and eggs. Add the breadcrumbs and continue mixing until combined.

Place the meatloaf mixture in the centre of the prepared tin. Wet your hands with cold water and form into a loaf shape about 15 cm/6 inches wide x 10 cm/4 inches high. Place in the centre of the preheated oven for 30 minutes.

Meanwhile, whisk together the sugar, ketchup, Dijon mustard and a pinch of salt in a small bowl to make the glaze.

After 30 minutes, remove the meatloaf from the oven and spread the glaze evenly over the top with a spoon. Return to the oven for 35–45 minutes, remove and leave to rest for at least 15 minutes before slicing and serving.

Turkey with Orange & Rice

serves 4

1 tbsp olive oil

1 onion, chopped

450 g/1 lb skinless lean turkey, cut into thin strips

300 ml/10 fl oz unsweetened orange juice

1 bay leaf

100 g/3½ oz small broccoli florets

1 large courgette, diced

1 large orange

450 g/1 lb cooked brown rice

Salt and black pepper, to taste

9–10 stoned black olives in brine, drained and quartered, to garnish

Shredded basil leaves, to garnish

Heat the oil in a large frying pan and cook the onion and turkey, stirring, for 4–5 minutes until lightly browned.

Pour in the orange juice, add the bay leaf and season to taste with salt and pepper. Bring to the boil and simmer for 10 minutes.

Meanwhile, bring a large saucepan of water to the boil and cook the broccoli florets, covered, for 2 minutes. Add the diced courgette, then bring back to the boil. Cover and cook for a further 3 minutes. Drain and set aside.

Using a sharp knife, peel the skin and white pith from the orange. Slice the orange to make thin circular slices, then halve each slice.

Stir the broccoli, courgette, rice and orange slices into the turkey mixture. Gently mix together and check the seasoning, then heat through for a further 3–4 minutes, or until the mixture is piping hot.

Transfer the turkey rice to warmed serving plates and serve garnished with black olives and shredded basil.

Macaroni & Tuna Layer

serves 4

280 g/10 oz dried macaroni

2 tbsp oil, plus extra for greasing

1 garlic clove, crushed

70 g/2½ oz white mushrooms, sliced

½ red pepper, thinly sliced

140 g/5 oz canned tuna in brine, drained and flaked

½ tsp dried oregano

2 tomatoes, sliced

2 tbsp dried breadcrumbs

55 g/2 oz mature Cheddar or Parmesan cheese, grated

Salt and black pepper, to taste

For the sauce

25 g/1 oz butter or margarine

1 tbsp plain flour

225 ml/8 fl oz milk

Salt and black pepper, to taste

Preheat the oven to 200°C/400°F/Gas Mark 6. Grease a 1-litre/1¾-pint ovenproof dish.

Bring a large saucepan of lightly salted water to the boil and cook the macaroni for 10–12 minutes or until tender. Drain, rinse and drain thoroughly.

Heat the remaining oil in a non-stick frying pan and fry the garlic, mushrooms and pepper until soft. Add the tuna, oregano and season to taste with salt and pepper, then heat through.

Add half the cooked macaroni to the prepared dish. Cover with the tuna mixture and then add the remaining macaroni.

To make the sauce, melt the butter in a saucepan over a medium–low heat, stir in the flour and cook for 1 minute. Add the milk gradually and bring to the boil, stirring constantly. Simmer for 1–2 minutes until thickened. Season to taste with salt and pepper. Pour the sauce over the macaroni.

Lay the sliced tomatoes over the sauce and sprinkle with the breadcrumbs and cheese. Bake for 25 minutes or until piping hot and the top is well browned.

Classic Beef Fajitas

serves 4-6

650 g/1 lb 7 oz beef tenderloin, cut into strips

6 garlic cloves, chopped

Juice of 1 lime

Pinch of chilli powder

Pinch of paprika

Pinch of ground cumin

1–2 tbsp vegetable oil, for frying

Salt and black pepper, to taste

For the pico de gallo salsa

8 ripe tomatoes, diced

3 spring onions, sliced

1–2 fresh green chillies, such as jalapeños, deseeded and chopped

3–4 tbsp chopped fresh coriander

5–8 radishes, diced

Ground cumin, to taste

Salt and black pepper, to taste

To serve

12 flour tortillas

1–2 avocados, stoned, peeled and sliced

115 g/4 oz soured cream

In a mixing bowl, combine the beef with the garlic, half the lime juice, the chilli powder, paprika and cumin. Season to taste with salt and pepper, mix well and marinate for at least 30 minutes at room temperature.

To make the pico de gallo salsa, combine the tomatoes in a bowl with the spring onions, chillies, coriander and radishes. Season to taste with cumin, salt and pepper. Set aside.

Heat a lightly greased non-stick frying pan over a medium heat and warm the tortillas one at a time. Once finished, wrap them in foil to keep them warm.

Add the oil to the frying pan and stir-fry the beef mixture over a high heat until browned and just cooked through.

Toss the avocado in the remaining lime juice and serve with the sizzling hot meat, warmed tortillas, pico de gallo salsa and soured cream.

Sausage & Beans

serves 4

8 sausages

3 tbsp olive oil

1 large onion, chopped

2 garlic cloves, chopped

1 green pepper, deseeded and sliced

400 g/14 oz canned chopped tomatoes

2 tbsp sun-dried tomato purée

425 g/15 oz canned cannellini beans

Mashed potatoes or rice, to serve

Prick the sausages all over with a fork. Heat 2 tablespoons of the oil in a large, heavy-based frying pan. Add the sausages and cook over a low heat, turning frequently, for 10–15 minutes until evenly browned and cooked through. Remove from the frying pan and keep warm. Drain off the oil and wipe out the pan with kitchen paper.

Heat the remaining oil in the frying pan. Add the onion, garlic and pepper and cook for 5 minutes, stirring occasionally, or until softened.

Add the tomatoes to the frying pan and let the mixture simmer, stirring occasionally, for about 5 minutes or until slightly reduced and thickened.

Stir the sun-dried tomato purée, cannellini beans and sausages into the mixture in the frying pan. Cook for 4–5 minutes, or until the mixture is piping hot. Add 4–5 tablespoons of water if the mixture becomes too dry.

Transfer the hot sausage and bean casserole to serving plates and serve with mashed potatoes or rice.

Fried Chicken with Tomato & Bacon Sauce

serves 4

25 g/1 oz butter

2 tbsp olive oil

4 skinless, boneless chicken breasts or 8 skinless, boneless chicken thighs

For the tomato & bacon sauce

25 g/1 oz butter

2 tbsp olive oil

1 large onion, finely chopped

2 garlic cloves, finely chopped

1 celery stick, finely chopped

4 bacon rashers, chopped

400 g/14 oz canned chopped tomatoes

2 tbsp tomato purée

Muscovado sugar, to taste

125 ml/4 fl oz water

1 tbsp chopped fresh basil

1 tbsp chopped fresh parsley, plus extra to garnish

Salt and black pepper, to taste

First, make the sauce. Melt the butter with the oil in a large saucepan over a low heat. Add the onion, garlic, celery and bacon and cook, stirring occasionally, for 5 minutes until softened. Stir in the tomatoes, tomato purée, sugar to taste and water, and season to taste with salt and pepper. Increase the heat to medium and bring to the boil, then reduce the heat and simmer, stirring occasionally, for 15–20 minutes until thickened.

In a large frying pan, melt the butter with the oil. Add the chicken and cook over a medium–high heat for 4–5 minutes on each side until evenly browned.

Stir the basil and parsley into the sauce. Add the chicken and spoon the sauce over it. Cover and simmer for 10–15 minutes until cooked through and tender. Garnish with parsley and serve immediately.

Baked Fish with Lime

serves 4

900 g/2 lb white fish fillets, such as sea bass or cod

1 lime, halved

3 tbsp extra virgin olive oil

1 large onion, finely chopped

3 garlic cloves, finely chopped

3 pickled jalapeño chillies, chopped

15 g/½ oz chopped fresh coriander

Salt and black pepper, to taste

Lemon and lime wedges, to serve

Preheat the oven to 180°C/350°F/Gas Mark 4.

Place the fish fillets in a bowl and season to taste with salt and pepper. Squeeze the juice from the lime over the fish.

Heat the olive oil in a non-stick frying pan. Add the onion and garlic and cook, stirring frequently, for 2 minutes, or until softened. Remove from the heat.

Place one third of the onion mixture and half of the chillies and coriander in the base of a shallow casserole or roasting tin. Arrange the fish on top. Top with the remaining onion mixture, chillies and coriander.

Bake for 15–20 minutes or until the fish has become slightly opaque and firm to the touch. Serve immediately, with lemon and lime wedges for squeezing over the fish.

Pork Chops & Spicy Beans

3 tbsp vegetable oil

4 lean pork chops

2 onions, thinly sliced

2 garlic cloves, crushed

2 fresh green chillies, deseeded and chopped

2.5-cm/1-inch piece of fresh ginger, peeled and chopped

1½ tsp cumin seeds

1½ tsp ground coriander

600 ml/1 pint stock or water

2 tbsp tomato purée

½ aubergine, trimmed and cut into 1-cm/ ½-inch dice

425 g/15 oz canned red kidney beans, drained

4 tbsp double cream

Salt and black pepper, to taste

Heat the oil in a large frying pan, add the pork chops and seal until browned on both sides. Remove from the frying pan and rest until required.

Add the onions, garlic, chillies, ginger and spices, and fry gently for 2 minutes. Stir in the stock, tomato purée and aubergine, and season to taste with salt and pepper.

Bring the mixture to the boil, place the pork chops on top, then cover and simmer gently over a medium heat for 30 minutes.

Remove the chops for a moment and stir the red kidney beans and double cream into the mixture. Return the chops to the frying pan, cover, and heat through for 5 minutes. Taste and adjust the seasoning if necessary. Serve hot.

Vegetable Lasagne

serves 4-6

1 aubergine, sliced

3 tbsp olive oil

2 garlic cloves, crushed

1 red onion, sliced

3 mixed peppers, deseeded and diced

140 g/5 oz mixed mushrooms, sliced

2 celery sticks, sliced

1 courgette, diced

½ tsp chilli powder

½ tsp ground cumin

2 tomatoes, chopped

300 g/10½ oz passata

2 tbsp chopped fresh basil

8 lasagne verde sheets

Salt and black pepper, to taste

For the cheese sauce

25 g/1 oz butter or margarine

1 tbsp plain flour

125 ml/4 fl oz vegetable stock

300 ml/10 fl oz milk

85 g/3 oz Cheddar cheese, grated

1 tsp Dijon mustard

1 tbsp chopped fresh basil

1 egg, beaten

Preheat the oven to 180°C/350°F/Gas Mark 4.

Place the aubergine slices in a colander, sprinkle with salt and leave to stand for 20 minutes. Rinse under cold water, drain and reserve.

Heat the oil in a large saucepan. Add the garlic and onion and sauté for 1–2 minutes. Add the peppers, mushrooms, celery and courgette and cook, stirring constantly, for 3–4 minutes. Stir in the chilli powder and cumin and cook for a further minute. Mix in the tomatoes, passata and basil, and season to taste with salt and pepper.

For the cheese sauce, melt the butter in a saucepan. Stir in the flour and cook for 1 minute. Remove from the heat and gradually stir in the stock and milk. Return to the heat and add half the cheese and the mustard. Boil, stirring, until thickened. Stir in the basil. Remove from the heat and stir in the egg.

Place half the lasagne sheets in a rectangular, ovenproof dish. Top with half the vegetable mixture and half the aubergine slices. Repeat the layers, then spoon the cheese sauce on top. Sprinkle with the remaining cheese and bake in the preheated oven for 40 minutes, or until golden. Serve immediately.

Gammon Cooked in Cider

serves 6

900 g/2 lb gammon

1 onion, halved

4 cloves

6 black peppercorns

1 tsp juniper berries (optional)

1 celery stick, chopped

1 carrot, sliced

750 ml/1¼ pints cider or apple juice

Place a rack in the slow cooker and stand the gammon on it. Stud each of the onion halves with two cloves and add to the cooker with the peppercorns, juniper berries, if using, celery and carrot.

Pour in the cider or apple juice, cover and cook on low for 8 hours until the meat is tender.

Remove the gammon from the cooker and place on a board. Cover with foil and leave to rest for 10–15 minutes. Discard the cooking liquid, reserving the vegetables.

Cut off any rind or fat from the gammon, then carve into slices and serve with the cooked vegetables.

Spaghetti Bolognese

1 tbsp olive oil

1 onion, finely chopped

2 garlic cloves, chopped

1 carrot, finely chopped

1 celery stick, finely chopped

55 g/2 oz pancetta, diced

350 g/12 oz lean steak mince

400 g/14 oz canned chopped tomatoes

2 tsp dried oregano

125 ml/4 fl oz red wine

2 tbsp tomato purée

400 g/14 oz fresh spaghetti

Salt and black pepper, to taste

Freshly grated Parmesan cheese, to serve

Heat the oil in a large frying pan. Add the onion and sauté for 3 minutes. Add the garlic, carrot, celery and pancetta, and sauté for 3–4 minutes or until the vegetables and pancetta are soft and just beginning to brown.

Add the steak mince and cook, stirring, over a high heat for a further 3 minutes, or until all of the meat is browned. Stir in the tomatoes, oregano and wine, and bring to the boil. Reduce the heat to low and simmer for 45 minutes. Stir in the tomato purée and season to taste with salt and pepper.

Bring a large saucepan of lightly salted water to the boil. Add the spaghetti, bring back to the boil and cook for 3–4 minutes, until tender but still firm to the bite. Drain thoroughly.

Transfer the spaghetti to a serving plate and pour the Bolognese sauce over the pasta. Toss to mix well and serve hot with the Parmesan cheese.

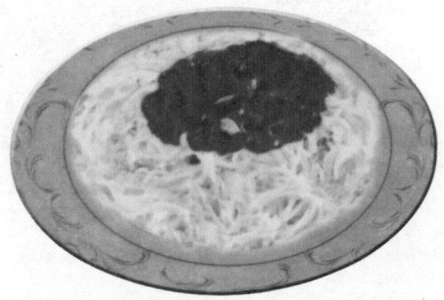

Chicken with Black-eyed Beans

serves 4

200 g/7 oz dried black-eyed beans, soaked overnight and drained

1 tsp salt

2 onions, finely chopped

2 garlic cloves, chopped

1 tsp ground turmeric

1 tsp ground cumin

1 x 1.25 kg/2 lb 12 oz whole chicken, cut into 8 pieces

1 green pepper, deseeded and chopped

2 tbsp olive oil

2.5-cm/1-inch piece of fresh ginger, grated

2 tsp coriander seeds

½ tsp fennel seeds

1 tbsp chopped fresh coriander, to garnish

Put the black-eyed beans into a wok or large saucepan with the salt, onions, garlic, turmeric and cumin. Cover with water, bring to the boil and cook for 15 minutes.

Add the chicken and pepper to the wok and bring to the boil. Reduce the heat and simmer for 30 minutes, or until the beans are cooked through and the chicken is tender and the juices run clear when a skewer is inserted into the thickest part of the meat.

Heat the oil in a separate wok or frying pan and stir-fry the ginger, coriander seeds and fennel seeds for 30 seconds.

Stir the fried spices into the chicken. Simmer for a further 5 minutes, garnish with the chopped coriander and serve immediately.

Slow Cooked Salmon

serves 4

150 ml/5 fl oz fish stock

225 ml/8 fl oz dry white wine

2 lemons

1 onion, thinly sliced

4 x 175 g/6 oz salmon fillets

1 tbsp dried mixed herbs

500 g/1 lb 2 oz spinach, coarse stalks removed

Freshly grated nutmeg, to taste

175 g/6 oz unsalted butter, plus extra for greasing

Salt and black pepper, to taste

Lightly grease a slow cooker pot with butter. In a small saucepan, combine the stock and wine and bring to the boil. In the meantime, thinly slice one of the lemons. Put half the lemon slices and all the onion slices over the base of the slow cooker pot and top with the salmon fillets. Season to taste with salt and pepper, add the mixed herbs and cover the fish with the remaining lemon slices. Pour the hot stock mixture over the fish, cover and cook on low for 1½ hours, until the fish flakes easily.

While the fish is cooking, grate the rind and squeeze the juice from the remaining lemon. When the fish is nearly ready, heat a deep saucepan over a medium–low heat and wilt the spinach in just the residual water clinging to the leaves. Drain well, squeezing out as much water as possible. Chop the spinach finely, arrange on warmed serving plates and season to taste with salt, pepper and nutmeg.

Carefully lift the fish out of the slow cooker and discard the lemon and onion slices. Place the salmon fillets on top of the spinach and keep warm.

Melt the butter in a small saucepan over a low heat. Stir in the lemon rind and half the juice. Taste and adjust the seasoning, adding more lemon juice, salt or pepper if needed. Pour the lemon butter sauce over the fish and serve immediately.

Roast Pork Loins with Black Cherry Sauce

serves 6

2 x 600-g/1-lb 5-oz trimmed pork loins

Coarse sea salt, to taste

4 tbsp black pepper

2 tbsp vegetable oil

1 garlic clove, crushed

5 tbsp balsamic vinegar

150 g/5½ oz black cherry jam

225 ml/8 fl oz chicken stock

25 g/1 oz cold unsalted butter

Preheat the oven to 190°C/375°F/Gas Mark 5.

Coat the pork fillets generously with the salt and black pepper. Heat the vegetable oil in a large ovenproof frying pan over a medium–high heat until it begins to smoke. Sear the pork on all sides for about 2 minutes until completely browned all over. Remove from the heat and place the pan in the centre of the preheated oven.

Roast the pork for 25 minutes, or until cooked through. When the pork is cooked, transfer to a plate and cover loosely with foil. Leave to rest while the sauce is made.

Pour off the excess fat from the frying pan and place over a high heat. Add the garlic and cook for just 15 seconds, then add the balsamic vinegar, black cherry jam and chicken stock. Cook, scraping the base of the pan with a wooden spoon to deglaze the pan drippings.

Boil for about 6–7 minutes, until the sauce reduces by about half. Turn off the heat and whisk in the cold butter, stirring constantly, until it dissolves. Taste and adjust the seasoning if necessary. Slice the pork and serve with the sauce generously spooned over.

Steak Topped with Mushrooms

serves 4

For the mushrooms

25 g/1 oz butter

4 tbsp olive oil

900 g/2 lb large button mushrooms, thickly sliced

2 garlic cloves, finely chopped

3 tbsp sherry vinegar

1 tbsp freshly chopped tarragon

Salt and black pepper, to taste

For the steak

4 x thick 300 g/10½ oz sirloin beef steaks

1 tbsp vegetable oil

4 tbsp chicken stock

1 tbsp butter

Salt and black pepper, to taste

4 jacket potatoes, to serve

4 tbsp soured cream, to serve

2 tbsp snipped fresh chives, to garnish

For the mushrooms, melt the butter and olive oil in a large frying pan over a medium–high heat. When the butter starts to sizzle, add the mushrooms and cook, stirring, for 10–15 minutes or until the mushroom juices have evaporated and they're well browned. Stir in the garlic and cook for 2 minutes.

Pour in the vinegar and, as soon as it starts to boil, turn off the heat. Transfer to a bowl and allow to cool to room temperature. Add the tarragon, salt and black pepper to taste. Reserve until needed.

Season the steaks generously on both sides with salt and pepper. Place a large heavy-based frying pan over a medium–high heat. Add the oil and, when hot, sear the steaks for about 5–6 minutes per side for medium–rare. Remove to a plate to rest.

Add the mushrooms to the frying pan. Add the stock and use a wooden spoon to scrape the base of the pan. Once the stock has deglazed the caramelized meat juices from the base of the pan, add the butter and stir until it dissolves. Taste and adjust the seasoning if necessary.

Place the steaks on warmed plates and spoon over the warm mushrooms. Serve immediately with jacket potatoes and soured cream, garnished with the chives.

Meatballs with Tomato Relish

1 onion, finely chopped

2 garlic cloves, finely chopped

2 tsp water

2 slices bread, crusts removed

450 g/1 lb lean steak mince

1 cooked baby beetroot, chopped

Pinch of paprika

2 tsp finely chopped fresh thyme

1 egg

Salt and black pepper, to taste

Sprigs of fresh thyme, to garnish

For the tomato relish

175 g/6 oz passata

2 tsp creamed horseradish

Preheat the oven to 230°C/450°F/Gas Mark 8.

To make the tomato relish, mix the passata and creamed horseradish together in a small bowl. Cover and set aside until required.

Put the onion, garlic and 2 teaspoons of water in a small saucepan and simmer over a low heat for 5 minutes. Increase the heat, bring to the boil and cook until all the water has evaporated. Remove from the heat.

Tear the bread into pieces and place in a small bowl. Add enough cold water to just cover and leave to soak for 5 minutes. Squeeze the excess water from the bread and place in a bowl with the steak mince, onion and garlic mixture, beetroot, paprika, thyme and egg. Season to taste with salt and pepper and mix thoroughly.

Form the mixture into 24 small balls between the palms of your hands. Thread three balls each onto eight metal skewers and place on a baking tray. Bake in the preheated oven for 10 minutes, or until well browned. Transfer to a serving dish, garnish with a few sprigs of thyme and serve with the tomato relish.

Chicken with Lime Stuffing

serves 4-6

1 x 2.25 kg/5 lb whole chicken

Olive oil, for brushing

1 large courgette

25 g/1 oz butter

Juice of 1 lime

Lime slices and shreds of lime rind, to garnish

For the stuffing

½ small courgette

175 g/6 oz low-fat soft cheese

Finely grated rind of 1 lime

2 tbsp fresh breadcrumbs

Salt and black pepper, to taste

Preheat the oven to 190°C/375°F/Gas Mark 5.

To make the stuffing, trim and roughly grate the courgette and mix with the cheese, lime rind, breadcrumbs and season to taste with salt and pepper.

Carefully ease the skin away from the breast of the chicken with your fingertips, taking care not to split it.

Push the stuffing under the skin to cover the breast evenly.

Place in a roasting tin, brush with oil and roast for 2 hours, or until the chicken is tender and the juices run clear when a skewer is inserted into the thickest part of the meat. While the chicken is cooking, trim the remaining courgette and cut into long, thin strips with a vegetable peeler or sharp knife. Heat a non-stick frying pan over a medium–low heat and sauté the courgette in the butter and lime juice until just tender, then serve with the chicken. Garnish the chicken with the lime slices and lime rind and serve immediately.

Prawns with Coconut Rice

serves 4

100 g/3½ oz dried Chinese mushrooms

2 tbsp vegetable or groundnut oil

6 spring onions, chopped

35 g/1¼ oz dessicated coconut

1 fresh green chilli, deseeded and chopped

200 g/7 oz Thai fragant rice

150 ml/5 fl oz fish stock

400 ml/14 fl oz canned coconut milk

350 g/12 oz cooked shelled prawns

6 sprigs fresh Thai basil

Place the mushrooms in a small bowl, cover with hot water and set aside to soak for 30 minutes. Drain, then cut off and discard the stalks and slice the caps.

Heat the oil in a wok and stir-fry the spring onions, dessicated coconut and chilli for 2–3 minutes until lightly browned. Add the mushrooms and stir-fry for 3–4 minutes.

Add the rice and stir-fry for 2–3 minutes, then add the stock and bring to the boil. Reduce the heat and add the coconut milk. Simmer for 10–15 minutes until the rice is tender and most of the liquid has been absorbed. Stir in the prawns and basil, heat through and serve.

Steak Mince in Tomato Sauce on a Bap

serves 4-6

600 g/1 lb 5 oz lean steak mince

½ onion, diced

2 garlic cloves, chopped

1 green pepper, deseeded and diced

475 ml/16 fl oz water

200 g/7 oz tomato ketchup

1½ tbsp muscovado sugar

1 tsp Dijon mustard

Dash of Worcestershire sauce

1½ tsp salt, or to taste

Cayenne pepper, to taste

6 baps or burger buns, to serve

Potato croquettes, to serve

Heat a large non-stick frying pan over a medium heat, add the steak mince and onion and cook, stirring, until the meat begins to brown. As it cooks, break the meat into very small pieces with a slotted spoon.

Add the garlic and green pepper and cook, stirring, for 2 minutes. Add half the water. Bring to a simmer, scraping the base of the pan to dissolve any browned bits.

Stir in the ketchup, sugar, mustard, Worcestershire sauce, salt, cayenne pepper to taste, and the remaining water. Bring to a simmer, reduce the heat to low and simmer for 30–45 minutes, or until most of the liquid has evaporated and the meat mixture is thick, rich and tender. Taste and adjust the seasoning. Serve hot on the baps accompanied by potato croquettes.

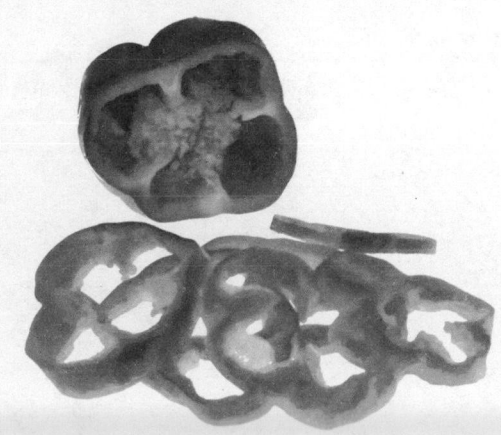

Pork & White Wine Stew

85 g/3 oz plain flour

1.3 kg/3 lb pork fillet, cut into 5-mm/¼-inch slices

4 tbsp corn oil

2 onions, thinly sliced

2 garlic cloves, finely chopped

400 g/14 oz canned chopped tomatoes

350 ml/12 fl oz dry white wine

1 tbsp torn fresh basil leaves

2 tbsp chopped fresh parsley

Salt and black pepper, to taste

Fresh oregano sprigs, to garnish

Fresh crusty bread, to serve

Spread the flour on a plate and season with salt and pepper. Coat the pork slices in the flour, shaking off any excess. Heat the oil in a flameproof casserole over a medium heat. Add the pork slices and cook, turning occasionally, for 4–5 minutes or until browned all over. Transfer the pork to a plate with a slotted spoon.

Add the onions to the casserole and cook over a low heat, stirring occasionally, for 10 minutes, or until golden brown. Add the garlic and cook for a further 2 minutes, then add the tomatoes, wine and basil, and season to taste with salt and pepper. Cook, stirring frequently, for 3 minutes.

Return the pork to the casserole, cover and simmer gently for 1 hour, or until the meat is tender. Add the parsley, garnish with oregano sprigs and serve immediately with fresh crusty bread.

Salt Beef & Cabbage

serves 6-10

1.3–2.25 kg/3 5 lb salt beef
1 tsp salt
2 tsp black pepper
1 tsp pickling spice
1 bay leaf
900 g/2 lb potatoes, cut into quarters
4 carrots, cut into chunks
1 onion, cut into large dice
3 celery sticks, cut into large dice
1 small white cabbage, cored and cut into 8 wedges
Farmhouse-style bread, to serve
Hot English mustard, to serve

Place the salt beef, the salt and pepper, pickling spice and bay leaf into a large saucepan with 3 litres/5¼ pints of cold water. Cover and bring to the boil over a high heat. Turn the heat down to low and simmer slowly for 2½ hours.

Add the potatoes, carrots, onion and celery. Simmer, covered, for 20 minutes. Add the cabbage and cook, covered, for a further 20 minutes or until the potatoes and vegetables are tender.

Remove the beef and leave to rest for 5 minutes, covered. Slice against the grain and serve with the vegetables, some of the cooking liquid, farmhouse-style bread and mustard.

Pasta with Bacon & Tomatoes

serves 4

900 g/2 lb small, ripe tomatoes

6 rindless smoked bacon rashers

55 g/2 oz butter

1 onion, chopped

1 garlic clove, crushed

4 sprigs fresh oregano, finely chopped

450 g/1 lb dried orecchiette

1 tbsp olive oil

Salt and black pepper, to taste

Freshly grated pecorino cheese, to serve

Score the tomatoes and blanch in boiling water. Drain, peel and deseed the tomatoes, then roughly chop the flesh. Set aside.

Using a sharp knife, chop the bacon into small pieces. Melt the butter in a frying pan. Add the bacon and fry over a medium heat until golden.

Add the onion and garlic and fry for 5–7 minutes until just softened.

Add the tomatoes and oregano to the pan and season to taste with salt and pepper. Reduce the heat and simmer for 10–12 minutes.

Bring a large saucepan of lightly salted water to the boil. Add the orecchiette and oil, and cook for 12 minutes until just tender but still firm to the bite. Drain the pasta and transfer to a warmed serving dish or bowl.

Spoon the hot bacon and tomato sauce over the pasta, toss to coat and serve with the pecorino cheese.

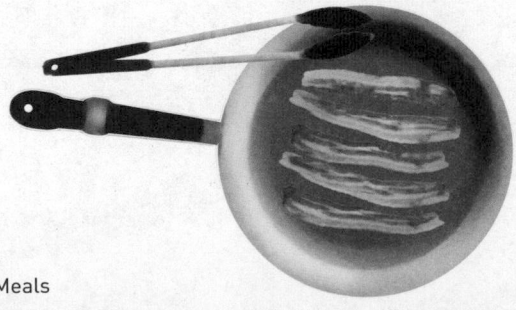

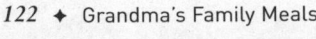

Potato, Leek & Chicken Pie

serves 4

225 g/8 oz waxy potatoes, cubed

70 g/2½ oz butter

175 g/6 oz skinless, boneless chicken breast, cubed

1 leek, sliced

125 g/4½ oz chestnut mushrooms, sliced

2½ tbsp plain flour

300 ml/10 fl oz milk

1 tbsp Dijon mustard

2 tbsp chopped fresh sage

225 g/8 oz filo pastry, thawed if frozen

40 g/1½ oz butter, melted

Salt and black pepper, to taste

Preheat the oven to 180°C/350°F/Gas Mark 4.

Bring a saucepan of lightly salted water to the boil and cook the potato cubes for 5 minutes. Drain and set aside.

Melt the butter in a large frying pan and cook the chicken for 5 minutes or until browned all over.

Add the leek and mushrooms and cook, stirring, for 3 minutes. Stir in the flour and cook, stirring constantly, for 1 minute. Gradually stir in the milk and bring to the boil. Add the mustard, sage and potato cubes, and simmer for 10 minutes. Season to taste with salt and pepper.

In the meantime, line a deep pie dish with half of the sheets of filo pastry. Spoon the sauce into the dish and cover with a sheet of pastry. Brush the pastry with melted butter and lay a further sheet on top. Brush this sheet with melted butter.

Cut the remaining filo pastry into strips and fold them on the top of the pie to create a ruffled effect. Brush the strips with melted butter and cook in the preheated oven for 45 minutes or until golden brown and crisp. Serve hot.

Layered Vegetable Bake

serves 4

1 tbsp olive oil, for brushing

650 g/1 lb 7 oz potatoes

2 leeks

2 beef tomatoes

8 fresh basil leaves

1 garlic clove, finely chopped

300 ml/10 fl oz vegetable stock

Salt and black pepper, to taste

Preheat the oven to 180°C/350°F/Gas Mark 4. Brush a large ovenproof dish with a little of the olive oil. Thinly slice the potatoes, trim and thinly slice the leeks, and slice the tomatoes.

Place a layer of potato slices in the base of the dish, sprinkle with half the basil leaves and cover with a layer of leeks. Top with a layer of tomato slices. Repeat these layers until all the vegetables are used up, ending with a layer of potatoes. Stir the chopped garlic into the vegetable stock and season to taste with salt and pepper. Pour the stock over the vegetables and brush the top with the remaining olive oil.

Bake in the preheated oven for 1½ hours, or until the vegetables are tender and the topping is golden brown. Serve immediately.

Barbecue Ribs

2 racks of pork ribs, trimmed of excess fat, patted dry

350 ml/12 fl oz barbecue sauce

For the rub

70 g/2½ oz packed muscovado sugar

3 tbsp coarse sea salt

1 tsp black pepper

1 tbsp smoked or regular paprika

½ tsp dried thyme

½ tsp dried mustard

½ tsp garlic powder

½ tsp onion powder

¼ tsp cayenne pepper

Combine the rub ingredients in a small bowl and mix thoroughly. Place each rack of ribs in the centre of a large piece of heavy-duty foil. Generously apply the dry rub to both sides of the two racks (more on the meat side). Wrap each rack in foil and transfer to the refrigerator for at least 4 hours or overnight.

Preheat the oven to 120°C/250°F/Gas Mark ½.

Put the two foil-wrapped racks on a baking tray and place in the preheated oven. Bake for 2 hours. Remove the ribs from the oven and, using tongs, carefully open the foil (excess fat can be poured off). Place both racks on one piece of the foil and brush the barbecue sauce generously on both sides.

Increase the oven temperature to 180°C/350°F/Gas Mark 4. Return the ribs to the oven. Continue cooking, brushing on more barbecue sauce several times for about 30–45 minutes, or until the ribs are tender and well glazed.

Remove and leave to rest for 5 minutes before cutting and serving. Ribs can be tossed in additional sauce if liked, or served with sauce on the side.

Chilli con Carne

serves 6-8

1 tbsp vegetable oil

1 large onion, diced

1 kg/2 lb 4 oz lean steak mince

3 garlic cloves, chopped

4 tbsp chilli powder

1 tbsp ground cumin

1 tsp black pepper, or to taste

½ tsp smoked paprika

¼ tsp cayenne pepper

1 tsp dried oregano

1 tsp sugar

1 large green pepper, deseeded and diced

1 large red pepper, deseeded and diced

425 g/15 oz passata

2 tbsp tomato purée

750 ml/1¼ pints water, or more as needed

425 g/15 oz canned pinto beans, drained and rinsed

425 g/15 oz canned kidney beans, drained and rinsed

Salt and pepper, to taste

Fresh coriander leaves, to garnish

Grated Cheddar cheese, to garnish

Add the vegetable oil and onion to a large, heavy-based saucepan. Place over a medium–high heat and sauté for 5 minutes, or until the onion begins to soften. Add the steak mince and cook for about 10 minutes. As the meat browns, use a wooden spoon to break it into small pieces.

Add the garlic, chilli powder, cumin, black pepper, smoked paprika, cayenne pepper, oregano and sugar. Cook, stirring, for 2 minutes.

Stir in the peppers, passata, tomato purée and water. Bring to a simmer, reduce the heat to medium–low and cook, uncovered, stirring occasionally, for 1 hour.

After an hour, stir in the beans and simmer for a further 30 minutes. If needed, add more water during the cooking to adjust the desired thickness. Season to taste with salt and pepper. Serve hot, garnished with grated Cheddar cheese and fresh coriander leaves.

Chicken & Parmesan Bake with Tomato Sauce

serves 6

6 x 175–200 g/6–7 oz skinless, boneless chicken breasts

2 tbsp olive oil

2 garlic cloves, chopped

Chilli flakes, to taste

1 kg/2 lb 4 oz passata

4 tbsp chopped basil

150 g/5½ oz mozzarella cheese, grated

70 g/2½ oz Parmesan cheese, grated

140 g/5 oz ready-prepared garlic croûtons

Salt and black pepper, to taste

For the sauce

1 onion, diced

1 celery stick, finely diced

4 tbsp olive oil

4 garlic cloves, finely chopped

1 tsp salt

2 tsp sugar

½ tsp dried Italian herbs

Pinch of chilli flakes

1 tsp anchovy paste

1 tsp white wine vinegar

1 tbsp tomato purée

550 g/1 lb 4 oz canned plum tomatoes

2 tbsp chopped fresh basil

Preheat the oven to 180°C/350°F/Gas Mark 4.

Place the chicken breasts on a plate and season to taste on both sides with salt and black pepper. Set aside.

Spread the olive oil, garlic and chilli flakes evenly over the base of a 33 x 23-cm/13 x 9-inch ovenproof casserole. Add a quarter of the passata and spread evenly. Place the chicken breasts in the dish and space evenly. Top with the rest of the passata and basil.

Top with half the mozzarella and half the Parmesan cheese. Pour over the croûtons and spread evenly. Top with the remaining cheese. Bake in the preheated oven for 40 minutes, or until the top is browned and the chicken is cooked through.

While the bake is cooking, make the sauce. Heat a saucepan over a medium heat and sweat the onions and celery in the olive oil for 5–6 minutes, or until translucent. Add the garlic and cook for a further minute. Add the salt, sugar, dried herbs, chilli flakes, anchovy paste, vinegar and tomato purée. Cook, stirring, for 2 minutes.

Add the tomatoes, bring to a simmer, turn the heat down to low and simmer gently, stirring occasionally, for 45 minutes. Water may be added to adjust the thickness. Taste and adjust the seasoning. Serve hot over slices of the chicken bake, garnished with the basil.

Wing Rib of Beef

1 wing rib of beef, about 4–8 ribs, trimmed and tied

55–115 g/2–4 oz butter, at room temperature

Coarse sea salt and black pepper, to taste

For the sauce

6 tbsp creamed horseradish

6 tbsp crème fraîche or soured cream

Place the rib in a large, sturdy roasting tin. No rack is needed as the bones form a natural rack. Rub the entire surface of the joint with the butter and season generously to taste with the salt and pepper. Leave the rib out at room temperature for 2 hours.

Preheat the oven to 230°C/450°F/Gas Mark 8.

Put the joint in the preheated oven for 20 minutes to sear the outside, then turn the temperature down to 160°C/325°F/Gas Mark 3 and roast for 15 minutes per 450 g/1 lb for rare or 20 minutes per 450 g/1 lb for medium. If you prefer well done, turn the temperature to 190°C/375°F/Gas Mark 5 instead and roast for 25 minutes per 450 g/1 lb.

Transfer to a serving platter and leave the joint to rest, loosely covered with foil, for at least 30 minutes before slicing.

For the sauce, mix together the creamed horseradish and crème fraîche in a small bowl. Serve with the sliced meat.

Spaghetti & Meatballs

serves 4-6

1 tbsp olive oil, plus extra for greasing

1 large onion, finely chopped

2 garlic cloves, finely chopped

900 g/2 lb steak mince

85 g/3 oz fresh white breadcrumbs

1 tsp dried Italian herbs

1 large egg, beaten

3 tbsp chopped fresh flat-leaf parsley

25 g/1 oz freshly grated Parmesan cheese, plus extra to serve

1–2 tsp salt, plus extra to taste

1 tsp freshly ground black pepper, plus extra to taste

900 g/2 lb prepared pasta sauce

150 ml/5 fl oz water

450–700 g/1–1 lb 9 oz dried spaghetti

Heat the olive oil in a frying pan and fry the onion and garlic for 6–7 minutes until softened but not brown. Transfer to a large mixing bowl and leave to cool. Preheat the oven to 220°C/425°F/Gas Mark 7. Grease a large baking tray.

Add the steak mince, breadcrumbs, dried herbs, egg, parsley, cheese and salt and pepper to the bowl, and mix thoroughly with clean wet hands. Divide and shape the mixture into about 54 walnut-sized meatballs. Place on the prepared baking tray and bake in the preheated oven for 20 minutes.

Heat the pasta sauce and water in a large pan. Add the hot meatballs and simmer gently for 25–30 minutes, stirring occasionally. Adjust the seasoning to taste.

Bring a very large saucepan of lightly salted water to the boil. Add the spaghetti, bring back to the boil and cook for 8–10 minutes, until tender but still firm to the bite. Drain well.

Ladle some of the sauce from the meatballs over the drained spaghetti and toss to coat. Serve topped with the meatballs, remaining sauce and some freshly grated Parmesan cheese.

Pork Casserole

100 g/3½ oz plain flour

1.3 kg/3 lb pork fillet, cut into 5-mm/¼-inch slices

4 tbsp vegetable oil

2 onions, thinly sliced

2 garlic cloves, finely chopped

400 g/14 oz canned chopped tomatoes

350 ml/12 fl oz dry white wine

1 tbsp torn fresh basil leaves

2 tbsp chopped fresh parsley, plus extra to garnish

Salt and black pepper, to taste

Fresh crusty bread, to serve

Spread the flour on a plate and season to taste with salt and pepper. Toss the pork slices in the flour to coat, shaking off any excess. Heat the oil in a flameproof casserole over a medium heat. Add the pork slices and cook until browned all over. Using a slotted spoon, transfer the pork to a plate.

Add the onions to the casserole and cook over a low heat, stirring occasionally, for 10 minutes or until golden brown. Add the garlic and cook, stirring, for 2 minutes, then add the tomatoes with their juice, the wine and basil leaves, and season to taste with salt and pepper. Cook, stirring frequently, for 3 minutes.

Return the pork to the casserole, cover and simmer gently for 1 hour, or until the meat is tender. Stir in the chopped parsley. Serve immediately, garnished with the parsley and some fresh crusty bread.

Braised Lamb Shanks

6 lamb shanks, about 2.5 kg/5 lb 8 oz in total

2 tbsp olive oil

½ tsp dried rosemary

½ tsp dried thyme

1 tbsp butter

1 onion, diced

1 celery stick, diced

1 large carrot, peeled and diced

1 tbsp flour

4 garlic cloves, chopped

125 ml/4 fl oz red wine

225 ml/8 fl oz chicken stock

1 tbsp balsamic vinegar

125 ml/4 fl oz water

Pinch of cinnamon

1 tsp chopped fresh rosemary leaves

Salt and black pepper, to taste

Sautéed potatoes, to serve

Preheat the oven to 230°C/450°F/Gas Mark 8.

Place the shanks in a deep baking dish or roasting tin large enough to fit all the shanks in one layer. Rub with the olive oil, dried rosemary and thyme. Season generously with salt and pepper on both sides. Roast for 30 minutes to brown the lamb.

In the meantime, melt the butter in a saucepan over a medium–high heat. Add the onion, celery and carrot, and cook for 6–7 minutes, or until the vegetables soften and the edges start to brown and caramelize. Stir in the flour and cook for 1 minute. Add the garlic and cook for a further minute. Stir in the wine. When the wine comes to the boil, stir in the chicken stock, balsamic vinegar, water, cinnamon and rosemary. Bring back to the boil, turn off the heat and reserve.

Once the lamb has browned, remove it from the oven and reduce the temperature to 160°C/325°F/Gas Mark 3. Pour over the sauce mixture and distribute evenly. Cover with foil, crimping the edges to form a tight seal. Return to the oven and roast for 1 hour, lift the foil, turn over the shanks, rewrap and cook for a further hour, or until tender. Transfer the lamb shanks to a large bowl and cover with foil to keep warm.

Pour the braising liquid into a saucepan and boil rapidly to reduce. Serve the sauce spooned over the lamb shanks, accompanied by the sautéed potatoes.

Spicy Pork & Rice

serves 4

225 g/8 oz basmati rice
600 ml/1 pint cold water
350 g/12 oz pork fillet
2 tsp Chinese five spice
4 tbsp cornflour
3 large eggs, beaten
2 tbsp muscovado sugar
2 tbsp vegetable oil
1 onion, diced
2 garlic cloves, crushed
2 carrots, diced
1 red pepper, deseeded and diced
150 g/5½ oz peas
25 g/1 oz butter
Salt, to taste

Rinse the rice under cold running water and place in a large saucepan. Add the cold water and a pinch of salt. Bring to the boil, cover, then reduce the heat to low and simmer for about 9 minutes, or until all of the liquid has been absorbed and the rice is light and fluffy.

In the meantime, slice the pork into very thin even-sized pieces, using a sharp knife. Set aside until required.

Whisk together the five spice, cornflour, one of the eggs and the sugar. Toss the pork in the mixture until coated.

Heat the oil in a large wok or frying pan. Add the pork and cook over a high heat until it is cooked through and crispy. Remove the pork from the wok with a slotted spoon and set aside until required.

Add the onion, garlic, carrots, pepper and peas to the wok and stir-fry for 5 minutes.

Return the pork to the wok together with the cooked rice and stir-fry for 5 minutes.

Heat the butter in a frying pan. Add the remaining beaten eggs and cook until set. Turn out onto a clean board and slice thinly. Toss the strips of egg into the rice mixture and serve immediately.

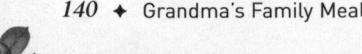

Creamy Pasta with Peas

serves 4

450 g/1 lb mixed plain and green dried tagliatelli or spaghetti

55 g/2 oz butter

900 g/2 lb fresh peas, shelled

175 ml/6 fl oz double cream

40 g/1½ oz freshly grated pecorino cheese, plus extra to serve

Pinch of freshly grated nutmeg

Salt and black pepper, to taste

Bring a large saucepan of lightly salted water to the boil. Add the pasta, bring back to the boil and simmer for 8–10 minutes until tender but still firm to the bite.

While the pasta is cooking, melt the butter in a heavy-based saucepan. Add the peas and cook over a low heat, stirring frequently, for 4–5 minutes. Pour in 125 ml/4 fl oz of the cream, bring to the boil and simmer for 1 minute.

When the pasta is cooked, drain well and add to the peas. Pour in the remaining cream, add the pecorino cheese and season to taste with nutmeg, salt and pepper. Toss well, then transfer to a warmed serving dish and serve immediately.

Chicken & Apple Bake

serves 4

4 x 175 g/6 oz mixed chicken pieces

1 tbsp olive oil

1 onion, chopped

2 celery sticks, coarsely chopped

1½ tbsp plain flour

300 ml/10 fl oz clear apple juice

150 ml/5 fl oz chicken stock

1 cooking apple, cored and cut into quarters

2 bay leaves

1–2 tsp clear honey

1 yellow pepper, deseeded and cut into chunks

1 tbsp butter, melted

1 large eating apple, cored and sliced

2 tbsp muscovado sugar

Salt and black pepper, to taste

1 tbsp chopped fresh mint, to garnish

Preheat the oven to 190°C/375°F/Gas Mark 5. Lightly rinse the chicken and pat dry with kitchen paper.

Heat the oil in a deep frying pan and cook the chicken over a medium–high heat, turning frequently, for 10 minutes or until golden and sealed. Using a slotted spoon, transfer to a casserole.

Add the onion and celery to the frying pan and cook over a medium heat, stirring frequently, for 5 minutes or until softened. Sprinkle in the flour and cook, stirring constantly, for 2 minutes, then remove from the heat. Gradually stir in the apple juice and stock, then return to the heat and bring to the boil, stirring. Add the cooking apple, bay leaves and honey and season to taste with salt and pepper.

Pour over the chicken in the casserole dish, then cover and cook in the preheated oven for 25 minutes. Add the pepper and cook for a further 10–15 minutes or until the chicken is tender and the juices run clear when a skewer is inserted into the thickest part of the meat.

Meanwhile, preheat the grill to high. Line the grill pan with foil. Brush the eating apple slices with half the melted butter, then sprinkle with a little sugar and cook under the grill for 2–3 minutes, or until the sugar has caramelized. Turn the slices over. Brush with the remaining butter, sprinkle with the remaining sugar, and cook for a further 2 minutes. Serve the bake with the apple slices and mint.

Turkey Escalopes

serves 4-6

200 g/7 oz plain flour

1 tsp garlic powder

1 tsp onion powder

¼ tsp cayenne pepper

4 large eggs

400 g/14 oz dried breadcrumbs, or more as needed

900 g/2 lb turkey escalopes, sliced or pounded to an even 5-mm/¼-inch thickness

1 tsp poultry seasoning

Rapeseed oil, for frying

Salt and black pepper, to taste

Lemon wedges, to serve

In a shallow dish, combine the flour, garlic powder, onion powder and cayenne pepper. Stir thoroughly and reserve. Whisk the eggs in another mixing bowl and reserve. Pour the breadcrumbs into a third shallow baking dish.

Season the turkey escalopes generously on both sides with the salt and pepper, and dust lightly with the poultry seasoning.

Dredge the turkey in the seasoned flour, then dip the escalopes into the egg and, once coated, transfer to the breadcrumbs. Turn over several times, pressing lightly into the breadcrumbs to ensure the meat is thoroughly coated. Transfer the escalopes to a plate while you finish breading the remaining escalopes. Once finished, leave to rest for 15 minutes before frying.

Pour about 5 mm/¼ inch of the oil into a large, heavy-based frying pan and set over a medium–high heat. When the oil reaches 180°C/350°F or a cube of bread browns in 30 seconds it is hot enough to start frying. Cook the escalopes for about 2–3 minutes per side, or until golden brown and cooked through.

Work in batches, drain on kitchen paper or a wire rack, and keep in a warm oven until all are done. Serve immediately with the lemon wedges.

Pot Roast Beef

1 x 2.25 kg/5 lb beef brisket

2 tbsp vegetable oil

1 tbsp butter

1 onion, diced

2 celery sticks, chopped

2 tbsp flour

3 garlic cloves, chopped

125 ml/4 fl oz red wine

2 tsp tomato purée

475 ml/16 fl oz beef stock

1 bay leaf

1 tsp dried thyme

½ tsp salt

600 g/1 lb 5 oz new potatoes

4 carrots, cut into large chunks

400 g/14 oz parsnips, cut into large chunks

1 tbsp butter, melted

Salt and black pepper, to taste

2 tbsp freshly chopped parsley, to garnish

Preheat the oven to 220°C/425°F/Gas Mark 7. Generously season the beef with salt and black pepper. Place a flameproof casserole over a high heat and add the vegetable oil. When the oil is hot, brown the beef very well for 5 minutes per side. Transfer the meat to a platter and reduce the heat to medium.

Add the butter, onion, celery and a pinch of salt. Sauté for 5 minutes to brown, then add the flour. Add the garlic and cook, stirring, for 1 minute. Whisk in the wine, scraping to deglaze the browned bits from the base of the pot. Add the tomato purée and pour in the beef stock.

Add the bay leaf, thyme and salt. When the liquid comes to a simmer, stir well and place the beef back into the dish. Turn the heat down to very low and simmer gently for about 45 minutes per 450 g/1 lb, or until tender. After 2 hours, carefully turn the beef over and continue cooking until done.

While the pot roast is cooking, prepare the vegetables. Place the potatoes, carrots and parsnips in a roasting tin. Skim a tablespoon of beef fat from the surface of the beef's braising liquid. Drizzle over the vegetables along with the melted butter. Toss the vegetables to coat and season with salt and pepper. Roast in the oven for 20 minutes, or until the vegetables are almost tender. Remove and reserve. About 30 minutes before the beef is done, uncover and add the vegetables to the dish. Continue cooking until the beef and vegetables are tender. Serve garnished with the parsley.

Chicken & Sausage Gumbo

serves 6

5 tbsp vegetable oil

40 g/1½ oz flour

1 onion, diced

3 celery sticks, diced

2 green peppers, deseeded and diced

30 g/1 oz spring onions, chopped

3 garlic cloves, crushed

450 g/1 lb spicy, smoked sausage, cut into 2.5-cm/1-inch pieces

1.5 litres/2½ pints chicken stock

280 g/10 oz canned chopped tomatoes

1 fresh green chilli, deseeded and finely chopped

650 g/1 lb 7 oz skinless, boneless chicken thighs, cut into 5-cm/2-inch pieces

1 tbsp Cajun seasoning

1 tsp salt

¼ tsp cayenne pepper, or to taste

½ tsp black pepper

450 g/1 lb okra, chopped

450 g/1 lb prawns, peeled and deveined

Cooked long grain rice, to serve (optional)

To make the roux, cook the oil and flour over a medium–low heat in a large heavy-based saucepan, stirring until it's a light, nutty brown colour.

Add the onion, celery and peppers to the roux and cook for a further 5 minutes to soften the vegetables. Add the spring onions, garlic and sausage, stir and cook for 3 minutes.

Add the stock, tomatoes, chilli, chicken, Cajun seasoning, salt, cayenne pepper and black pepper. Bring to the boil, reduce the heat to low and simmer, stirring occasionally, for 1 hour. Stir in the okra and simmer for a further 30 minutes, or until the chicken is very tender.

Stir in the prawns and cook for 3–4 minutes or until cooked through. Adjust the seasoning and spices, to taste. Serve hot with cooked rice, if using.

Stuffed Pork with Prosciutto

serves 4

500 g/1 lb 2 oz lean pork fillet

Small bunch fresh basil leaves

2 tbsp freshly grated Parmesan cheese

2 tbsp sun-dried tomato purée

6 thin slices prosciutto

1 tbsp olive oil

Salt and black pepper, to taste

For the tapenade

70 g/2½ oz stoned black olives

2 garlic cloves

4 tbsp olive oil

Preheat the oven to 190°C/375°F/Gas Mark 5.

Trim away any excess fat and membrane from the pork. Slice the pork lengthways down the centre, taking care not to cut all the way through.

Open out the pork and season the inside to taste with salt and pepper. Lay the basil leaves down the centre. Mix the cheese and sun-dried tomato purée in a bowl and spread over the basil leaves.

Press the pork back together. Wrap the prosciutto around the pork, overlapping to seal. Place on a rack in a roasting tray, seam-side down, and brush with the oil. Bake in the preheated oven for 30–40 minutes depending on the thickness, until cooked through. Leave to rest for 10 minutes.

For the tapenade, place all the ingredients in a blender or food processor and blend until smooth. Alternatively, for a coarser paste, finely chop the olives and garlic, and mix with the oil.

Drain the cooked pork, slice thinly and serve with the tapenade.

Buttermilk Fried Chicken

serves 6–8

1 x 1.8 kg/4 lb whole chicken, cut into 8 pieces

2 litres/3½ pints groundnut or vegetable oil, for frying

For the marinade

1 tsp salt

1 tsp black pepper

1 tsp paprika

½ tsp cayenne pepper

½ tsp white pepper

1 tsp poultry seasoning

475 ml/16 fl oz buttermilk

For the seasoned flour

250 g/9 oz plain flour

1 tbsp salt

1 tsp black pepper

1 tsp paprika

½ tsp cayenne pepper

½ tsp white pepper

1 tsp garlic salt

1 tsp onion powder

Place the chicken in a large glass bowl or plastic container. Add all the dry marinade ingredients and toss to coat very thoroughly. Pour over the buttermilk. Use tongs to move the chicken pieces around until they are coated. Cover and refrigerate for 6–12 hours.

Mix together the seasoned flour ingredients in a large baking dish. Drain the chicken pieces in a colander and toss in the flour to coat the chicken completely. Make sure it's thoroughly covered, including all the nooks and crannies. Gently shake off excess flour and transfer to a plate.

Heat the oil in a large, heavy-based saucepan to 180°C/350°F, or until a cube of bread browns in 30 seconds. Carefully add the chicken and fry for 10 minutes. Use tongs or a wire strainer to turn the pieces over, and continue cooking for a further 8–10 minutes or until crisp, golden brown and the juices run clear when a skewer is inserted into the thickest part of the meat.

Drain on a wire rack for 5 minutes. Check the seasoning and serve.

Smothered Pork Chops

4 large pork chops, about 4 cm/1½ inch thick

1 tsp poultry seasoning

2 tbsp vegetable oil

1 tbsp butter

1 large onion, sliced

4 garlic cloves, finely chopped

1 rounded tbsp flour

350 ml/12 fl oz chicken stock

4 tbsp buttermilk

4 tbsp water

Salt and black pepper, to taste

600 g/1 lb 5 oz cooked rice, to serve (optional)

Season the pork chops on both sides with the poultry seasoning, salt and pepper. Heat the oil in a large frying pan over a medium–high heat. When the oil is hot, brown the pork chops well for about 5 minutes per side. Transfer to a plate and reserve.

Pour off the excess oil and place the pan back on the hob over a medium heat. Add the butter and the onion along with a big pinch of salt. Sauté for about 10 minutes, or until the onion is well browned. The onion needs to caramelize for best results.

Stir in the garlic and cook for 1 minute. Stir in the flour and cook for 2 minutes. Add the chicken stock, buttermilk and water. As the mixture comes to a simmer, use a wooden spoon to scrape any browned bits from the base of the pan.

Reduce the heat to low and leave the onion gravy to gently simmer for 15 minutes. Add a splash of water if it seems to be getting too thick. Add the pork chops and any juices back to the pan, and coat with the gravy. Cook for about 10 minutes or until the pork is tender. Taste for seasoning and adjust if needed. Serve the pork chops over rice, if using, topped with the onion gravy.

Spicy Tomato Tagliatelle

serves 4

40 g/1½ oz butter

1 onion, finely chopped

1 garlic clove, crushed

2 small red chillies, deseeded and diced

450 g/1 lb fresh tomatoes, peeled, deseeded and diced

175 ml/6 fl oz vegetable stock

2 tbsp tomato purée

1 tsp sugar

400 g/14 oz fresh green and white tagliatelle

Salt and black pepper, to taste

Melt the butter in a large saucepan over a medium heat. Add the onion and garlic and cook for 3–4 minutes, or until softened.

Add the chillies to the pan and continue cooking for about 2 minutes.

Add the tomatoes and stock, reduce the heat and simmer, stirring, for 10 minutes.

Pour the sauce into a food processor and blend for 1 minute, until smooth. Alternatively, push the sauce through a sieve.

Return the sauce to the pan and add the tomato purée, sugar, and salt and pepper to taste. Gently heat through over a low heat until piping hot.

Bring a large saucepan of lightly salted water to the boil and cook the tagliatelle for 3–4 minutes or until tender but still firm to the bite. Drain the tagliatelle, transfer to serving plates and serve with the pasta sauce.

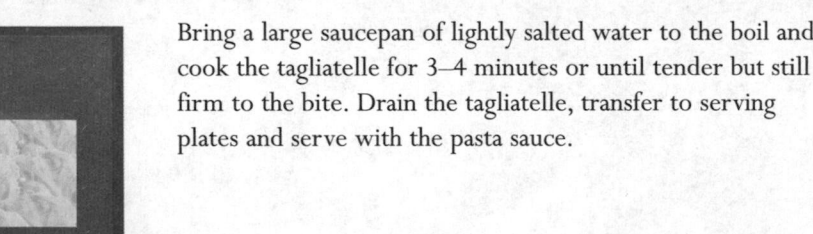

Pan-cooked Chicken

serves 4

4 chicken breasts, part boned

2 tbsp olive oil

25 g/1 oz butter

2 red onions, cut into wedges

2 tbsp lemon juice

150 ml/5 fl oz dry white wine

150 ml/5 fl oz chicken stock

2 tsp plain flour

425 g/15 oz canned artichoke hearts, drained and halved

Salt and pepper, to taste

Chopped fresh parsley, to garnish

Season the chicken with salt and pepper to taste. Heat the oil and half of the butter in a large frying pan. Add the chicken and fry for 4–5 minutes on each side until lightly golden. Remove from the frying pan using a slotted spoon.

Toss the onion in the lemon juice and add to the frying pan. Gently fry, stirring, for 3–4 minutes until just beginning to soften.

Return the chicken to the frying pan. Pour in the wine and stock, bring to the boil, cover and simmer gently for 30 minutes.

Remove the chicken from the frying pan, reserving the cooking juices, and keep warm. Bring the juices to the boil, and boil rapidly for 5 minutes to reduce the liquid.

Blend the remaining butter with the flour to form a paste. Reduce the juices to a simmer and spoon the paste into the frying pan, stirring, until thickened.

Adjust the seasoning according to taste, stir in the artichoke hearts and cook for a further 2 minutes. To serve, pour the mixture over the chicken and garnish with the parsley.

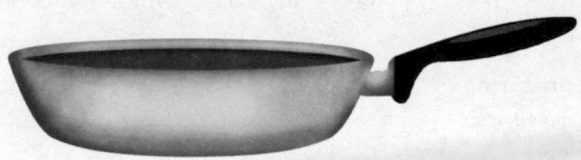

Slow-roasted Pork with Barbecue Sauce

serves 6-8

1 x 1.3–1.8 kg/3–4 lb pork shoulder

Burger buns or baps, to serve

Grated Cheddar cheese, to serve

For the dry rub

2 tbsp muscovado sugar

1 tbsp salt

1 tbsp black pepper

1 tbsp paprika

2 tsp chilli powder

2 tsp garlic powder

2 tsp onion powder

2 tsp ground cumin

1 tsp cayenne pepper

For the sauce

500 ml/17 fl oz ketchup

150 ml/5 fl oz dark treacle

125 ml/4 fl oz white wine vinegar

1 tsp paprika

1 tsp chilli powder

1 tsp Tabasco sauce

½ tsp black pepper

½ tsp salt

½ tsp ground cinnamon

½ tsp ground mixed spice

½ tsp ground mace

Preheat the oven to 110°C/225°F/Gas Mark ¼.

Rinse the meat and pat dry with kitchen paper. Trim off any large pieces of excess fat. Mix the rub ingredients together in a small bowl, and thoroughly coat the pork.

Place the pork, fattier-side up, in a large casserole. Pour 5 tablespoons of water into a small ovenproof ramekin. Place this ramekin in the casserole next to the meat. As the pork roasts, this will introduce moisture to the cooking environment. Cover tightly with the lid and place in the centre of the preheated oven.

Roast the pork for 12 hours, or until very tender. Turn the oven off and allow the pork to rest for 1 hour before removing.

To serve, place the pork on a chopping board and use two forks to pull it apart into small pieces.

For the sauce, whisk together all the ingredients in a saucepan. Bring to a simmer over a medium–low heat. Cook, stirring, for 3 minutes. Remove from the heat and leave to cool to room temperature before storing in an airtight container in the refrigerator. Serve the pork warm in burger buns topped with the sauce and grated cheese.

Braised Thin Ribs of Beef

serves 4

4 bacon rashers, cut into 1-cm/½-inch pieces

8 thin ribs of beef

1 large onion, diced

1 celery stick, diced

4 garlic cloves, chopped

2 tbsp flour

225 ml/8 fl oz dry sherry wine

750 ml/1¼ pints beef or veal stock

2 tsp tomato purée

6 sprigs fresh thyme

1 bay leaf

Salt and black pepper, to taste

Preheat the oven to 180°C/350°F/Gas Mark 4.

Add the bacon to a large heavy-based saucepan and fry over a medium heat until the fat is rendered out. Remove the bacon with a slotted spoon and reserve, leaving the fat in the pan.

Turn the heat up to medium–high and brown the ribs very well on all sides. Remove the ribs and reserve. Add the onion and celery, reduce the heat to medium and sauté for about 5 minutes until the onion is soft.

Add the garlic and flour and cook, stirring, for 2 minutes. Whisk in the sherry, turn the heat up to high and bring to the boil, scraping off any browned bits from the bottom of the pan. Add the beef stock, tomato purée, thyme, bay leaf, bacon, ribs and ½ teaspoon of salt.

When the liquid begins to simmer, cover tightly and place in the oven. Braise for 2 hours, or until the meat is tender, skimming any excess fat from the top as needed. Taste and adjust the seasoning. Serve the ribs with the cooking juices spooned over.

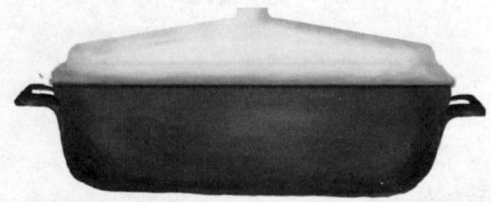

Stuffed Garlic Chicken

serves 4

4 chicken breasts, part-boned

115 g/4 oz frozen spinach, thawed

175 g/6 oz low-fat ricotta cheese

2 garlic cloves, crushed

1 tbsp olive oil

1 onion, chopped

1 red pepper, deseeded and sliced

400 g/14 oz canned chopped tomatoes

6 tbsp wine or chicken stock

10 stuffed olives, sliced

Salt and black pepper, to taste

Sprigs of fresh parsley, to garnish

Pasta, to serve

Preheat the oven to 200°C/400°F/Gas Mark 6.

Make a slit between the skin and meat on one side of each chicken breast. Carefully lift the skin to form a pocket, taking care to leave the skin attached to the other side.

Place the spinach in a sieve and press out the water with a spoon. Mix with the ricotta, half the garlic and season to taste with salt and pepper.

Spoon the spinach mixture under the skin of each chicken breast, then secure the edge of the skin with a cocktail stick.

Heat the oil in a large frying pan, add the onion and cook for a minute, stirring. Add the remaining garlic and the pepper and cook for 2 minutes. Stir in the tomatoes, wine, olives, and salt and pepper to taste. Set the sauce aside and chill the chicken if preparing in advance.

Bring the sauce to the boil, pour into an ovenproof dish and arrange the chicken breasts on top in a single layer.

Cook, uncovered, in the preheated oven for 35 minutes, or until the chicken is tender and the juices run clear when a skewer is inserted into the thickest part of the meat.

Spoon a little of the sauce over the chicken breasts, then transfer to serving plates and garnish with the parsley. Serve with pasta.

Beef & Vegetable Stew with Corn Cobs

serves 4

450 g/1 lb braising beef

1½ tbsp plain flour

1 tsp hot paprika

1–1½ tsp chilli powder

1 tsp ground ginger

2 tbsp olive oil

1 large onion, cut into chunks

3 garlic cloves, sliced

2 celery sticks, sliced

2 large carrots, chopped

300 ml/10 fl oz lager

300 ml/10 fl oz beef stock

450 g/1 lb potatoes, chopped

1 red pepper, deseeded and chopped

2 corn cobs, halved

6 tomatoes, cut into quarters

150 g/5½ oz shelled fresh or frozen peas

Salt and black pepper, to taste

Trim any fat from the beef and cut into 2.5-cm/1-inch chunks. Mix the flour and spices together. Toss the beef in the spiced flour until well coated.

Heat the oil in a large, heavy-based saucepan and cook the onion, garlic and celery, stirring frequently, for 5 minutes or until softened. Add the beef and cook over a high heat, stirring frequently, for 3 minutes or until browned on all sides and sealed.

Add the carrots, then remove from the heat. Gradually stir in the lager and stock, then return to the heat and bring to the boil, stirring. Reduce the heat, then cover and simmer, stirring occasionally, for 1½ hours.

Add the potatoes to the pan and simmer for a further 15 minutes. Add the red pepper and corn cobs and simmer for 15 minutes, then add the tomatoes and peas and simmer for a further 10 minutes, or until the beef and vegetables are tender. Season to taste with salt and pepper, and serve.

Chinese Chicken & Rice

1 tbsp dry sherry

2 tbsp light soy sauce

2 tbsp dark soy sauce

2 tsp muscovado sugar

1 tsp salt

1 tsp sesame oil

900 g/2 lb skinless, boneless chicken breast, diced

1 litre/1¾ pints chicken stock

25 g/1 oz mushrooms, sliced

40 g/1½ oz canned water chestnuts, drained and halved

70 g/2½ oz broccoli florets

1 yellow pepper, deseeded and sliced

4 tsp grated fresh ginger

125 g/4½ oz long-grain rice

Whole chives, to garnish

Mix together the sherry, soy sauces, sugar, salt and sesame oil in a mixing bowl.

Stir the chicken into the soy mixture, turning to coat well. Leave to marinate for about 30 minutes.

Bring the stock to the boil in a saucepan or preheated wok. Add the chicken with the marinade, mushrooms, water chestnuts, broccoli, pepper and ginger.

Stir in the rice, reduce the heat, cover and cook for 25–30 minutes until the chicken and vegetables are cooked through and the rice has absorbed the liquid. Transfer to serving plates, garnish with the chives and serve.

Pot Roast Lamb

serves 4

1 x 1.3–1.8 kg/3-4 lb leg of lamb

3–4 sprigs of fresh rosemary, plus extra to garnish

6 bacon rashers

4 tbsp olive oil

2–3 garlic cloves, crushed

2 onions, sliced

2 carrots, sliced

2 celery sticks, sliced

300 ml/10 fl oz dry white wine

1 tbsp tomato purée

300 ml/10 fl oz lamb or beef stock

2–3 tomatoes, peeled, cut into quarters and deseeded

1 tbsp chopped fresh parsley

1 tbsp chopped fresh oregano or marjoram

Salt and black pepper, to taste

Sprigs of fresh rosemary, to garnish

Preheat the oven to 180°C/350°F/Gas Mark 4.

Season the lamb to taste with salt and pepper. Lay the sprigs of rosemary over the lamb, cover evenly with the bacon rashers and tie in place with kitchen string. Heat the oil in a large frying pan and fry the lamb for about 10 minutes, turning several times. Remove the lamb from the frying pan and set aside.

Transfer the oil from the frying pan to a large flameproof casserole and cook the garlic and onions for 3–4 minutes until they begin to soften. Add the carrots and celery, and cook for a further 2 minutes.

Lay the lamb on top of the vegetables and press down to partially submerge the meat. Pour the wine over the lamb, add the tomato purée and simmer for 3–4 minutes. Add the stock, tomatoes and herbs, and season to taste with salt and pepper. Bring back to the boil for a further 3–4 minutes.

Cover the casserole tightly and cook in the preheated oven for 2–2½ hours until the lamb is very tender.

Remove the lamb from the casserole and take off the bacon and herbs along with the string if preferred. Keep warm. Strain the cooking juices and serve in a jug. Arrange the vegetables around the lamb, or serve in a separate dish. Garnish with the sprigs of rosemary.

Pot Roast Pork

serves 4-6

1 tbsp vegetable oil

55 g/2 oz butter

1 kg/2 lb 4 oz boned and rolled pork loin

4 shallots, chopped

2 fresh thyme sprigs, plus extra to garnish

150 ml/5 fl oz cider

150 ml/5 fl oz chicken stock or water

8 celery sticks, chopped

2 tbsp plain flour

150 ml/5 fl oz double cream

Salt and black pepper, to taste

Freshly cooked peas, to serve

Heat the oil with half the butter in a heavy-based saucepan or flameproof casserole. Add the pork and cook over a medium heat, turning frequently, for 5–10 minutes or until browned. Transfer to a plate.

Add the shallots to the pan and cook, stirring frequently, for 5 minutes or until softened. Add the thyme sprigs and return the pork to the pan with any juices that have collected on the plate. Pour in the cider and stock, season to taste with salt and pepper, then cover and simmer for 30 minutes. Turn the pork over and add the celery. Cover the pan and cook for a further 40 minutes.

In the meantime, make a paste by mashing the remaining butter with the flour in a small bowl. Transfer the pork and celery to a platter with a slotted spoon and keep warm. Remove and discard the thyme. Whisk the paste, a little at a time, into the simmering cooking liquid. Cook, stirring constantly, for 2 minutes, then stir in the cream and bring to the boil.

Slice the pork and spoon a little of the sauce over it. Garnish with thyme sprigs and serve immediately with the celery, peas and remaining sauce.

Chicken & Autumn Vegetable Bake

serves 4

3 tbsp olive oil

2 leeks, sliced

2 garlic cloves, sliced

2 x 175 g/6 oz large chicken breasts, cut into bite-sized pieces

2 sweet potatoes, cut into chunks

2 parsnips, scrubbed and sliced

1 red pepper, deseeded and cut into strips

1 yellow pepper, deseeded and cut into strips

100 g/3½ oz mixed wild mushrooms, cleaned

450 g/1 lb coarsely chopped tomatoes

600 g/1 lb 5 oz cooked white long-grain rice

1 small bunch fresh parsley, chopped

115 g/ 4 oz mature Cheddar cheese, grated

Salt and black pepper, to taste

Preheat the oven to 180°C/350°F/Gas Mark 4.

Heat the oil in a large frying pan over a medium heat, then add the leeks and garlic and cook, stirring frequently, for 3–4 minutes or until softened.

Add the chicken and cook, stirring frequently, for 5 minutes. Add the sweet potatoes and parsnips and cook, stirring frequently, for 5 minutes or until golden and beginning to soften. Add the peppers and mushrooms and cook, stirring frequently, for 5 minutes.

Stir in the tomatoes, rice and parsley, and season to taste with salt and pepper.

Spoon the mixture into an ovenproof dish. Scatter over the Cheddar cheese and bake in the preheated oven for 20–25 minutes. Serve immediately.

Fried Steak with White Gravy

serves 4

4 x 175 g/6 oz beef top round steaks

2 eggs, beaten

4 tbsp milk

125 g/4½ oz plain flour

1 tbsp paprika

½ tsp white pepper

Salt and black pepper, to taste

Vegetable oil as needed

For the gravy

115 g/4 oz sausage meat, or sausages with casing removed

3 spring onions, light parts chopped, green parts sliced and reserved

40 g/1½ oz butter

30 g/1 oz plain flour

600 ml/1 pint cold milk

Salt and black pepper, to taste

Pinch of cayenne pepper

Tenderise the beef by pounding with a meat mallet, then season both sides generously with salt and pepper.

Whisk together the eggs and milk in a shallow dish and reserve. Add the flour, paprika and white pepper to a second shallow dish and mix well to combine.

One at a time, dip the steaks into the egg mixture, turning to coat completely, and then dredge in the flour, coating both sides. Place the egged and floured steaks on a plate, and allow to rest for 10 minutes.

Add about 5 mm/¼ inch of vegetable oil to a large frying pan and place over a medium–high heat. When the oil begins to shimmer, add the steaks and cook for 3–4 minutes per side until golden brown and cooked through. Remove and drain for a couple of minutes on a wire rack set over some kitchen paper. If working in batches, keep the cooked steaks in a warm oven while you cook the rest.

To make the gravy, lightly brown the sausage meat in a medium saucepan over a medium heat. As it cooks, break the meat up into very small pieces with a wooden spoon. Add the light parts of the spring onion and the butter, and sauté for a few minutes until the onions are translucent.

Stir in the flour and cook for 3 minutes. Whisk in the cold milk gradually until combined. The gravy will thicken as it comes up to a simmer. Once simmering, reduce the heat to low and cook, stirring occasionally, for 15 minutes. Season to taste with salt, pepper and cayenne, and serve garnished with the reserved spring onions.

4

Grandma's Sweet Treats

Mocha Layer Cake

serves 8

Oil or melted butter, for greasing

250 g/9 oz self-raising flour

¼ tsp baking powder

4 tbsp cocoa powder

115 g/4 oz caster sugar

2 eggs

2 tbsp golden syrup

150 ml/5 fl oz sunflower oil

150 ml/5 fl oz milk

Filling and topping

1 tsp instant coffee

1 tbsp boiling water

300 ml/10 fl oz double cream

2 tbsp icing sugar

To decorate

50 g/1¾ oz chocolate shavings

Chocolate caraque

Icing sugar, for dusting

Preheat the oven to 180°C/350°F/Gas Mark 4. Grease three 18-cm/7-inch sandwich cake tins and line with greaseproof paper.

Sift the flour, baking powder and cocoa into a large mixing bowl. Stir in the caster sugar. Make a well in the centre and stir in the eggs, syrup, oil and milk. Beat with a wooden spoon, gradually mixing in the dry ingredients.

Divide the mixture between the prepared tins. Bake in the preheated oven for 35–45 minutes, or until springy to the touch. Leave the cakes to cool in their tins for 5 minutes, then turn out onto wire racks to cool completely.

For the filling and topping, dissolve the instant coffee in the boiling water and whip in a bowl with the cream and icing sugar until the cream is just holding its shape. Use half of the cream to sandwich the three cakes together. Spread the rest over the top and sides of the cake.

To decorate, lightly press the chocolate shavings into the cream around the edges of the cake. Transfer to a serving plate. Lay the caraque over the top of the cake. Cut a few thin strips of baking paper and place on top of the caraque to form a pattern. Dust lightly with icing sugar, then carefully remove the paper and serve.

Butter Shortbread Wedges

makes 8

115 g/4 oz butter, softened, plus extra for greasing
3 tbsp caster sugar
2 tbsp icing sugar
250 g/9 oz plain flour
Pinch of salt
2 tsp orange flower water or grated orange zest

Preheat the oven to 150°C/300°F/Gas Mark 2.

Lightly grease a shallow 20-cm/8-inch round cake tin.

In a large mixing bowl, cream together the butter, caster sugar and icing sugar until light and fluffy.

Sift the flour and salt into the creamed mixture. Add the orange flower water and bring everything together to form a soft dough.

On a lightly floured surface, roll out the dough to a 20-cm/ 8-inch round and place in the tin. Mark out eight evenly spaced lines on the dough for cutting into wedges once cooked.

Bake for 30–35 minutes, or until the shortbread is pale, golden and crisp.

Let the shortbread cool before removing the wedges from the tin. Store in an airtight container.

Double Fudge Brownies

makes 8-10

225 g/8 oz plain chocolate (with 70% cocoa solids), broken or chopped into small pieces

70 g/2½ oz butter, sliced into pieces, plus extra for greasing

200 g/7 oz caster sugar

¼ tsp salt

2 tbsp water

2 large eggs

1 tsp vanilla extract

90 g/3¼ oz plain flour

55 g/2 oz walnuts, chopped (optional)

Preheat the oven to 160°C/325°F/Gas Mark 3 and lightly grease a 20-cm/8-inch square baking dish.

Place the chocolate, butter, sugar, salt and water in a small saucepan over a very low heat. Heat, stirring often, until the chocolate and butter are melted.

Pour into a mixing bowl. Beat in the eggs one at a time. Stir in the vanilla extract and then the flour. Stir in the nuts, if using.

Pour into the prepared baking dish and bake for 35 minutes. Cool completely before cutting into squares.

Chocolate & Orange Ring

170 g/6 oz butter, softened, plus extra for greasing

150 g/5½ oz sugar

3 eggs, beaten

150 g/5½ oz self-raising flour, sifted

30 g/1 oz cocoa powder, sifted

5–6 tbsp orange juice

Grated zest of 1 orange

Preheat the oven to 180°C/350°F/Gas Mark 4.

Lightly grease a 25-cm/10-inch ring tin.

In a mixing bowl, cream together the butter and sugar with an electric whisk for about 5 minutes.

Add the beaten egg a little at a time, whisking well after each addition.

Using a metal spoon, fold the flour into the creamed mixture carefully, then spoon half the mixture into a separate mixing bowl.

Fold the cocoa powder and half the orange juice into one bowl and mix gently. Fold the orange zest and remaining orange juice into the other bowl and mix gently.

Place spoonfuls of each of the mixtures alternately into the ring, then drag a skewer through the mixture to create a marbled effect.

Bake in the preheated oven for 30–35 minutes, or until well risen and a skewer inserted in the centre comes out clean.

Let the cake cool in the tin before turning out onto a wire rack to cool completely.

Flapjacks

makes 20

225 g/8 oz butter
200 g/7 oz soft brown sugar
125 g/4½ oz golden syrup
400 g/14 oz porridge oats

Preheat the oven to 180°C/350°F/Gas Mark 4. Line a 23-cm/9-inch square cake tin with baking paper.

Put the butter, sugar and syrup into a saucepan and heat over a low heat for 2–3 minutes until melted. Mix in the porridge oats and stir well.

Pour the mixture into the prepared tin, press down well and bake in the centre of the preheated oven for 30–35 minutes until golden brown but still moist and slightly soft when pressed.

Remove from the oven and leave to cool for 5 minutes. Cut into squares and leave to cool completely for about 30 minutes in the tin.

Carefully remove the squares from the tin and store in an airtight container in a cool place for up to 3–4 days.

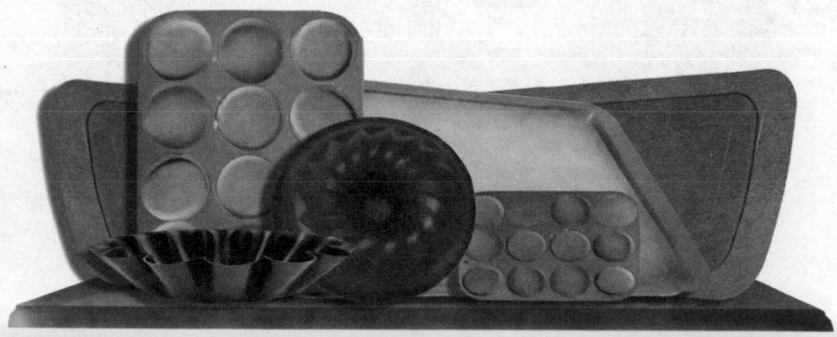

Cherry Pie

serves 8

For the pastry

125 g/4½ oz plain flour

¼ tsp baking powder

½ tsp mixed spice

½ tsp salt

55 g/2 oz caster sugar

55 g/2 oz unsalted butter, plus extra for greasing

1 egg, beaten, plus extra for glazing

For the filling

600 g/1 lb 5 oz stoned fresh cherries or drained canned cherries

100 g/3½ oz caster sugar

½ tsp almond extract

2 tsp cherry brandy

¼ tsp mixed spice

2 tbsp cornflour

2 tbsp water

Preheat the oven to 220°C/425°F/Gas Mark 7. Grease a 23-cm/9-inch round flan tin.

To make the pastry, sift the flour and baking powder into a large bowl. Stir in the mixed spice, salt and sugar. Rub in the butter with your fingertips until the mixture resembles fine breadcrumbs. Add the beaten egg and mix to a firm dough. Cut the dough in half and roll each half into a ball. Roll out one half of the dough and line the tin.

To make the filling, put half the cherries and the sugar in a large saucepan. Bring to a simmer over a low heat, stirring, until the sugar has dissolved. Stir in the almond extract, brandy and mixed spice. In a separate bowl, mix the cornflour and water to form a paste. Remove the saucepan from the heat, stir in the cornflour paste, then return to the heat and stir constantly until the mixture boils. Stir in the remaining cherries and pour into the pastry case.

Cut the remaining dough into long strips about 1 cm/½ inch wide. Lay five strips evenly across the top of the filling. Now lay six strips widthways over the strips, folding back every other strip each time you add a further widthways strip, to form a lattice. Trim off the ends and seal the edges with water. Use your fingers to crimp around the rim, then brush the top with beaten egg to glaze.

Cover with foil and bake in the preheated oven for 30 minutes. Discard the foil, then bake for a further 15 minutes, or until the crust is golden.

Blackberry & Apple Cake

serves 8-10

1 tbsp butter, for greasing

2 large cooking apples, peeled and diced

3 tbsp lemon juice

250 g/9 oz wholemeal flour

2½ tsp baking powder

1 tsp ground cinnamon, plus extra for dusting

150 g/5½ oz blackberries, thawed if frozen, plus extra for decorating

225 g/8 oz muscovado sugar

1 egg, beaten lightly

175 g/6 oz low-fat natural yogurt

55 g/2 oz granulated sugar

One small apple, sliced, for decorating

Preheat the oven to 190°C/375°F/Gas Mark 5.

Grease a 900-g/2-lb loaf tin with a little butter and line with baking paper. Place the prepared cooking apples in a saucepan with the lemon juice. Place them in a saucepan with the lemon juice, bring to the boil, cover and simmer for 10 minutes until soft. Beat well to form a paste. Set aside to cool.

Sift the flour, baking powder and cinnamon into a bowl, adding any bran that remains in the sifter. Stir in 100 g/3½ oz of the blackberries and the muscovado sugar.

Make a well in the centre of the ingredients and add the egg, yogurt and cooled apple paste. Mix until thoroughly blended. Spoon the mixture into the prepared loaf tin and level over the top with a palette knife.

Sprinkle with the remaining blackberries, pressing them down into the cake mixture, and top the mixture with the granulated sugar. Bake in the preheated oven for 40–45 minutes, then leave to cool in the tin.

Turn the cake out and peel away the baking paper. Serve dusted with cinnamon and decorated with the apple slices.

Almond Biscuits

100 g/3½ oz unblanched almonds

225 g/8 oz butter, softened

50 g/1¾ oz icing sugar, plus extra for sifting

250 g/9 oz plain flour

2 tsp vanilla extract

½ tsp almond extract

Preheat the oven to 180°C/350°F/Gas Mark 4.

Line two baking trays with greaseproof paper. Finely chop the almonds, or process them in a small food processor, taking care not to over-process them into a paste. Set aside.

Place the butter in a large mixing bowl and beat with an electric whisk until smooth. Sift in the icing sugar and continue beating until creamed and smooth.

Sift the flour into the bowl and beat in until blended. Add the vanilla and almond extracts and beat again to form a soft dough. Stir in the chopped almonds.

Using a teaspoon, shape the dough into 32 round balls about the size of walnuts. Place on the prepared baking trays, spaced well apart. Bake in the preheated oven for 20–25 minutes until set and just starting to turn golden brown.

Once cooked, leave the biscuits to stand on the baking trays for 2 minutes to firm up. Sift a thick layer of icing sugar over them. Transfer to a wire rack and leave to cool completely.

Lightly dust with more icing sugar just before serving. Store the biscuits in an airtight container for up to a week.

Pecan Pie

For the pastry
225 g/8 oz plain flour, plus extra for dusting
115 g/4 oz butter
2 tbsp caster sugar

For the filling
70 g/2½ oz butter
55 g/2 oz muscovado sugar
150 ml/5 fl oz golden syrup
2 large eggs, beaten
1 tsp vanilla extract
100 g/3½ oz pecan nuts

Preheat the oven to 200°C/400°F/Gas Mark 6.

For the pastry, sift the flour into a bowl and rub in the butter using your fingertips until it resembles fine breadcrumbs. Stir in the caster sugar and add enough cold water to mix to a firm dough. Wrap in clingfilm and chill in the refrigerator for 15 minutes until firm enough to roll out.

Roll out the dough on a lightly floured work surface and use to line a 23-cm/9-inch round, loose-based flan tin. Prick the base with a fork. Chill for 15 minutes.

Place the flan tin on a baking tray, line with a sheet of baking paper and fill with baking beans. Bake in the preheated oven for 10 minutes. Remove the paper and beans, and bake for a further 5 minutes. Reduce the oven temperature to 180°C/350°F/Gas Mark 4.

For the filling, place the butter, muscovado sugar and golden syrup in a saucepan and heat gently until melted. Remove from the heat and quickly beat in the eggs and vanilla extract.

Roughly chop the pecans and stir into the mixture. Pour into the tart case and bake for 35–40 minutes until the filling is just set. Serve warm or cold.

Whoopie Pies

makes 8

250 g/9 oz plain flour

3 tbsp cocoa powder

½ tsp bicarbonate of soda

¼ tsp salt

115 g/4 oz unsalted butter, softened

225 g/8 oz muscovado sugar

1 large egg

1¼ tsp vanilla

125 ml/4 fl oz buttermilk

For the filling

32 large marshmallows

4 tsp golden syrup

115 g/4 oz softened cream cheese

Preheat the oven to 190°C/375°F/Gas Mark 5. Line two baking trays with baking paper.

Sift the flour, cocoa powder, bicarbonate of soda and salt into a mixing bowl. Stir the mixture with a whisk to combine and aerate. Reserve until needed.

Add the butter and muscovado sugar to another large mixing bowl, and beat with an electric whisk until light and fluffy. Beat in the egg and vanilla until thoroughly combined.

Add a third of the flour mixture and stir until combined. Add half the buttermilk and stir until combined, then add half the remaining flour and stir. Add the remaining buttermilk, stir and then mix in the remaining flour.

Spoon the mixture onto the prepared baking trays, forming 16 discs about 1 cm/½ inch high and 7.5 cm/3 inches wide. You should fit about eight per tray. Bake for 12–14 minutes, or until the tops look cooked and are slightly firm to the touch. Remove and leave to rest for 15 minutes on the baking trays. Transfer to wire racks to cool completely.

For the filling, heat the marshmallows and golden syrup in a heatproof bowl set over a saucepan of simmering water. In another bowl, beat the cream cheese until fluffy. Fold in the marshmallow mixture and spread spoonfuls of the filling onto the flat sides of half the cakes. Top the iced halves with the remaining cake halves to form sandwiches, then serve.

Cheesecake with Fruit Sauce

serves 8-10

115 g/4 oz butter

200 g/7 oz digestive biscuits, finely crushed

1 tbsp sugar

900 g/2 lb soft cheese

150 g/5½ oz caster sugar

2 tbsp plain flour

1 tsp vanilla extract

Finely grated zest of 1 orange

Finely grated zest of 1 lemon

3 eggs

2 egg yolks

300 ml/10 fl oz double cream

For the sauce

115 g/4 oz berries, such as blackberries or raspberries

2 tbsp water

2–3 tbsp caster sugar

2 tbsp fruit liqueur, such as crème de cassis or crème de framboise

Preheat the oven to 180°C/350°F/Gas Mark 4.

Place a small saucepan over a low heat and melt the butter. Remove from the heat. Stir in the crushed biscuits and the 1 tablespoon of sugar. Stir well to combine. Press the biscuit mixture into the base of a 23-cm/9-inch cake tin. Place in the preheated oven and bake for 10 minutes. Remove and leave to cool.

Increase the oven temperature to 200°C/400°F/Gas Mark 6.

Using an electric whisk, beat the cream cheese until creamy, then gradually add the sugar and flour, and beat until smooth. Beat in the vanilla extract, orange and lemon zest then, one at a time, beat in the eggs and egg yolks. Finally, beat in the cream. The mixture should be light and fluffy.

Grease the sides of the cake tin and pour in the filling. Transfer to the preheated oven and bake for 15 minutes. Reduce the heat to 100°C/200°F/Gas Mark ¼ and bake for a further 30 minutes. Turn the oven off and leave to cool for 2 hours. Cover and refrigerate overnight.

For the sauce, put all the ingredients into a small, heavy-based saucepan and heat gently until the sugar has dissolved and the fruit juices run. Process to a paste in a food processor, then push through a non-metallic sieve into a serving bowl to remove the seeds. Add more sugar if necessary and serve warm or cold.

Chocolate Chip Biscuits

makes 30

280 g/10 oz plain flour

1 tsp bicarbonate of soda

1 tsp salt

225 g/8 oz butter, at room temperature

175 g/6 oz muscovado sugar

175 g/6 oz caster sugar

1 tsp vanilla extract

2 large eggs

350 g/12 oz plain chocolate chips

100 g/3½ oz walnuts, chopped (optional)

Preheat the oven to 190°C/375°F/Gas Mark 5.

Sift the flour, bicarbonate of soda and salt into a small mixing bowl. Whisk together briefly to combine. In a separate bowl, use an electric whisk to beat the butter, muscovado sugar, caster sugar and vanilla extract until light and creamy.

Add the eggs, one at a time, beating thoroughly after each addition. Stir in the flour mixture until combined. Stir in the chocolate chips and nuts, if using. Drop tablespoons of the biscuit dough onto ungreased baking trays, spaced well apart.

Bake in the preheated oven for 10 minutes, or until lightly browned around the edges. Allow to sit on the baking trays for 2 minutes, then transfer to wire racks to cool completely.

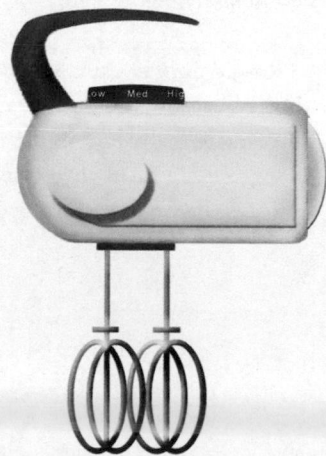

Carrot Cake
with Cream Cheese Icing

250 g/9 oz plain flour

1 tsp salt

2 tsp baking powder

1 tsp bicarbonate of soda

2 tsp cinnamon

½ tsp ground ginger

400 g/14 oz caster sugar

350 ml/12 fl oz vegetable oil

4 large eggs

55 g/2 oz butter, melted

225 g/8 oz carrots, grated

225 g/8 oz canned crushed pineapple, drained

55 g/2 oz chopped pecan nuts

55 g/2 oz chopped walnuts

Sugar paste carrots, to decorate (optional)

For the icing

115 g/4 oz unsalted butter, softened

225 g/8 oz cream cheese, softened

1 tbsp milk

1 tsp vanilla extract

450 g/1 lb icing sugar

Preheat the oven to 180°C/350°F/Gas Mark 4. Lightly grease a 33 x 23-cm/13 x 9-inch baking tin.

Whisk together the flour, salt, baking powder, bicarbonate of soda, cinnamon and ginger in a mixing bowl for 1–2 minutes. Reserve until needed.

In a separate mixing bowl, combine the sugar, oil and eggs, then use an electric whisk to mix until thoroughly combined. Whisk in the melted butter. Use a palette knife to stir in the carrots, pineapple and nuts. Stir in the flour mixture in two additions.

Use a spatula to scrape the mixture into the prepared baking tin. Bake in the preheated oven for about 40 minutes, or until the top springs back slightly when gently touched. Remove from the oven and allow to cool completely before icing.

To make the icing, use an electric whisk to beat together the butter, cream cheese, milk and vanilla extract until light and fluffy. Gradually beat in the icing sugar to form a smooth icing. Spread evenly over the cooled cake. Decorate with sugar paste carrots, if using.

Spiced Apple Ring

serves 8

175 g/6 oz butter, softened, plus extra for greasing

175 g/6 oz caster sugar

3 eggs, lightly beaten

150 g/5½ oz self-raising flour

1 tsp ground cinnamon

1 tsp ground mixed spice

2 apples, cored and grated

2 tbsp apple juice or milk

25 g/1 oz flaked almonds

Preheat the oven to 180°C/350°F/Gas Mark 4. Lightly grease a 25-cm/10-inch ring tin.

In a mixing bowl, cream together the butter and sugar until light and fluffy. Gradually add the beaten eggs, beating well after each addition.

Sift the flour and spices, then carefully fold into the creamed mixture with a figure-of-eight movement.

Stir in the grated apples and the apple juice and mix to a soft dropping consistency.

Sprinkle the flaked almonds around the base of the tin and spoon the cake mixture on top. Level the surface with the back of the spoon.

Bake in the preheated oven for about 30 minutes until well risen and a skewer inserted into the centre comes out clean.

Let the cake cool in the tin before turning out and transferring to a wire rack to cool completely. Cut into slices and serve.

Millionaire's Shortbread

makes 8-10

200 g/7 oz plain flour

115 g/4 oz butter, cut into small pieces, plus extra for greasing

3 tbsp muscovado sugar, sifted

For the topping

40 g/1½ oz butter, softened

3 tbsp muscovado sugar

400 ml/14 fl oz canned condensed milk

125 g/4½ oz milk chocolate, broken into pieces

Preheat the oven to 190°C/375°F/Gas Mark 5.

Grease a 23 x 23 x 4-cm/9 x 9 x 1½-inch square cake tin.

Sift the flour into a mixing bowl and rub in the butter with your fingers until the mixture resembles fine breadcrumbs. Add the sugar and mix to form a firm dough.

Press the mixture into the base of the prepared tin and prick all over with a fork. Bake in the preheated oven for 20 minutes, or until lightly golden. Leave to cool in the tin.

To make the topping, place the butter, sugar and condensed milk into a non-stick saucepan and cook over a gentle heat, stirring constantly, until the mixture comes to the boil.

Reduce the heat and cook for 4–5 minutes until the caramel is pale golden and thick and is coming away from the sides of the pan. Pour the topping over the shortbread base and leave to cool.

When the caramel topping is firm, melt the milk chocolate in a heatproof bowl set over a saucepan of simmering water. Spread the melted chocolate over the topping, leave it to set in a cool place, then cut the shortbread into squares to serve.

Peanut Butter Cookies

makes 12-15

200 g/7 oz plain flour
½ tsp baking powder
½ tsp salt
250 g/9 oz creamy peanut butter
115 g/4 oz butter, at room temperature
1¼ tsp vanilla extract
100 g/3½ oz muscovado sugar
100 g/3½ oz granulated sugar
2 eggs

Preheat the oven to 180°C/350°F/Gas Mark 4.

Sift together the flour, baking powder and salt in a mixing bowl and reserve. In a large mixing bowl, beat the peanut butter, butter and vanilla extract together until smooth. Add the sugars and beat for a further minute. Beat in the eggs one at a time. Mix in the flour in two additions.

Wrap the dough in clingfilm and refrigerate for at least 2 hours. Once chilled, roll or scoop the dough into 4-cm/1½-inch balls, and place on an ungreased baking tray, spaced well apart.

Use a fork to flatten each ball by making a criss-cross pattern. Bake in the preheated oven for 15 minutes or until golden. Remove the cookies from the oven and allow to cool on the baking tray for 5 minutes. Transfer to a wire rack with a palette knife to cool completely before serving.

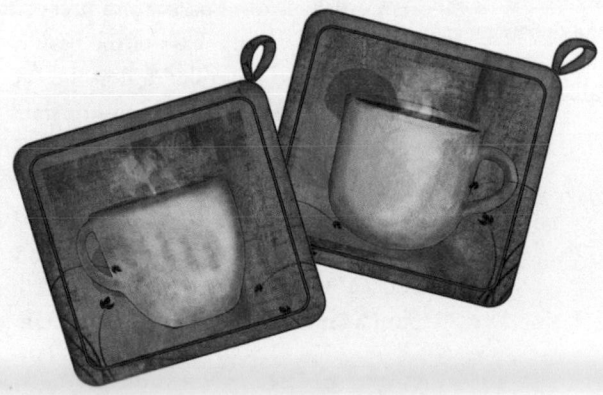

Sweet Potato Pie

serves 8-10

For the pastry

150 g/5½ oz plain flour, plus extra for dusting

½ tsp salt

¼ tsp sugar

20 g/¾ oz butter, diced

3 tbsp vegetable suet

2–2½ tbsp ice-cold water

For the filling

450 g/1 lb orange-fleshed sweet potatoes

3 large eggs, beaten

100 g/3½ oz muscovado sugar

350 ml/12 fl oz canned evaporated milk

40 g/1½ oz butter, melted

2 tsp vanilla extract

1 tsp ground cinnamon

1 tsp ground nutmeg or freshly grated nutmeg

½ tsp salt

Preheat the oven to 220°C/425°F/Gas Mark 7.

To make the pastry, sift the flour, salt and sugar into a bowl. Add the butter and suet to the bowl and rub in with your fingertips until fine crumbs form. Sprinkle over 2 tablespoons of the water and mix with a fork until a soft dough forms. Add ½ tablespoon of water if the dough is too dry. Wrap in clingfilm and chill in the refrigerator for at least 1 hour.

Meanwhile, bring a large saucepan of water to the boil over a high heat. Add the sweet potatoes and cook for 15 minutes. Drain, then cool them under cold running water. When cool, peel and mash them. Beat in the eggs and sugar until very smooth and then beat in the remaining ingredients. Set aside until required.

Roll out the dough on a lightly floured work surface into a thin 28-cm/11-inch round and line a 23-cm/9-inch pie tin. Trim off the excess pastry and press a floured fork around the edges. Prick the base of the pastry case all over with the fork and place crumpled foil in the centre. Bake in the preheated oven for 12 minutes or until lightly golden.

Remove the pastry case from the oven and discard the foil. Pour in the sweet potato filling and return to the oven for a further 10 minutes. Reduce the oven temperature to 160°C/325°F/Gas Mark 3 and bake for 35 minutes, or until a knife inserted in the centre comes out clean.

Rich Apple Scones

makes 8

250 g/9 oz self-raising flour, plus extra for dusting

1 tbsp sugar

Pinch of salt

115 g/4 oz butter, cut into small pieces, plus extra for greasing

1 apple, peeled, cored and chopped

1 egg, beaten

2 tbsp treacle

5 tbsp milk

Preheat the oven to 220°C/425°F/Gas Mark 7 and lightly grease a baking tray.

Sift the flour, sugar and salt into a mixing bowl. Rub in the butter with your fingertips until the mixture resembles fine breadcrumbs.

Stir the chopped apple into the mixture until combined.

In another bowl, mix together the beaten egg, treacle and milk. Add to the dry ingredients to form a soft dough.

On a lightly floured work surface, roll out the dough to a thickness of 2 cm/¾ inch and cut out eight scones, using a 5-cm/2-inch plain pastry cutter.

Arrange the scones on the baking tray and bake in the preheated oven for 8–10 minutes.

Transfer the scones to a wire rack and cool slightly before serving. Serve the scones split in half and spread with butter.

Marbled Loaf Cake

serves 8-10

125 g/4½ oz plain chocolate, broken into pieces

3 tbsp milk

70 g/2½ oz butter, plus extra for greasing

100 g/3½ oz caster sugar

1 egg, beaten

3 tbsp soured cream

125 g/4½ oz self-raising flour

½ tsp baking powder

½ tsp vanilla extract

Preheat the oven to 160°C/325°F/Gas Mark 3.

Grease a 900-g/2-lb loaf tin and line with baking paper.

To melt the chocolate, combine in a small heatproof bowl with the milk and set the bowl over a saucepan of simmering water. Heat gently until just melted. Remove from the heat.

In another bowl, cream together the butter and sugar until light and fluffy. Beat in the egg and soured cream. Sift the flour and baking powder over the mixture, then fold in using a metal spoon.

Spoon half the mixture into a separate bowl and stir in the melted chocolate. Add the vanilla to the plain mixture.

Spoon the chocolate and vanilla mixtures alternately into the prepared loaf tin, swirling lightly with a knife for a marbled effect. Bake in the preheated oven for 40–45 minutes, or until well risen and a skewer inserted in the centre comes out clean.

Once cooked, cool in the tin for 10 minutes, then transfer to a wire rack to cool completely.

Chequerboard Biscuits

makes 18

175 g/6 oz butter, softened, plus extra for greasing

60 g/2¼ oz icing sugar

1 tsp vanilla extract or grated rind of ½ orange

280 g/10 oz plain flour

55 g/2 oz plain chocolate

1 egg white, beaten

Preheat the oven to 180°C/350°F/Gas Mark 4. Lightly grease two baking trays.

Beat the butter and icing sugar in a mixing bowl until light and fluffy. Beat in the vanilla extract. Gradually beat in the flour to form a soft dough. Use your fingers to incorporate the last of the flour and bring the dough together.

Put the chocolate in a heatproof bowl set over a saucepan of gently simmering water and heat until melted. Divide the dough in half and beat the melted chocolate into one half. Keeping each half of the dough separate, cover and chill in the refrigerator for 30 minutes.

Roll out each piece of dough to a rectangle measuring 20 x 7.5 cm/8 x 3 inches long and 4 cm/1½ inches thick. Brush one piece of dough with a little egg white and place the other on top.

Cut the block of dough in half lengthways and turn over one half. Brush the side of one block of dough with egg white and push the other on top of it, so that it resembles a chequerboard.

Cut the block into thin slices and place each slice flat on the prepared baking trays, spaced well apart.

Bake in the preheated oven for 10 minutes until just firm. Cool on the baking trays for a few minutes before transferring to a wire rack to cool completely.

Chocolate Marshmallow Cake

serves 6

85 g/3 oz unsalted butter

200 g/7 oz caster sugar

½ tsp vanilla extract

2 eggs, lightly beaten

85 g/3 oz plain chocolate, broken into pieces

150 ml/5 fl oz buttermilk

150 g/5½ oz self-raising flour

½ tsp bicarbonate of soda

Pinch of salt

55 g/2 oz milk chocolate, grated, for decorating

For the icing

175 g/6 oz white marshmallows

1 tbsp milk

2 egg whites

2 tbsp sugar

Preheat the oven to 160°C/325°F/Gas Mark 3. Grease a 15 x 5-cm/6 x 2-inch round cake tin and line it with baking paper.

Beat together the butter, sugar and vanilla extract in a bowl until pale and fluffy, then gradually beat in the eggs.

Melt the plain chocolate in a heatproof bowl set over a saucepan of simmering water. When the chocolate has melted, stir in the buttermilk gradually, until well combined. Remove from the heat and leave to cool slightly.

Sift together the flour, bicarbonate of soda and salt into a separate bowl.

Add the chocolate mixture and the flour mixture alternately to the creamed mixture a little at a time until combined. Spoon the mixture into the cake tin and smooth the surface. Bake in the preheated oven for 50 minutes until a skewer inserted into the centre of the cake comes out clean. Turn out onto a wire rack to cool.

Meanwhile, make the icing. Put the marshmallows and milk in a small saucepan and heat very gently until the marshmallows have melted. Remove the pan from the heat and leave to cool a little. Stir in the egg whites and sugar and mix well. Spread the icing over the cake and decorate with the grated chocolate.

Sticky Pecan Pie Bars

makes 8

For the base
200 g/7 oz plain flour

115 g/4 oz butter, diced and left at room temperature for 30 minutes, plus extra for greasing

55 g/2 oz caster sugar

For the topping
2 large eggs

85 g/3 oz light muscovado sugar

4 tbsp golden syrup

25 g/1 oz butter, melted

½ tsp vanilla extract

75 g/2½ oz pecan nuts, roughly chopped

Preheat the oven to 180°C/350°F/Gas Mark 4. Grease a 20-cm/8-inch square shallow cake tin and line the base and sides with greaseproof paper.

To make the base, place the flour and butter in a large bowl. Using your fingertips, rub the butter into the flour until the mixture resembles fine breadcrumbs. Stir in the sugar and knead the mixture together with your hands to form large clumps.

Spoon the mixture into the prepared tin and press down firmly with the back of a spoon to form an even layer. Prick all over with a fork. Bake in the preheated oven for 25–30 minutes until pale golden. Leave to cool for 15 minutes.

To make the topping, place the eggs and sugar in a large mixing bowl and whisk together lightly. Whisk in the golden syrup, melted butter and vanilla extract, and stir in the pecan nuts. Pour the mixture over the base in the tin and bake in the oven for 25–30 minutes until just set and golden brown. Leave to cool completely in the tin. When cold, remove from the tin and cut into eight bars to serve.

Lemon & Sesame Seed Cookies

2 tbsp sesame seeds

225 g/8 oz butter, softened

140 g/5 oz caster sugar

1 tbsp finely grated lemon rind

1 egg yolk, lightly beaten

280 g/10 oz plain flour

Pinch of salt

For the icing

115 g/4 oz icing sugar

Few drops of lemon extract

1 tbsp hot water

Dry-fry the sesame seeds in a heavy-based frying pan over a low heat, stirring frequently, for 2–3 minutes. Remove from the heat and leave to cool.

Place the butter, sugar, lemon rind and toasted seeds in a large bowl and beat together until light and fluffy, then beat in the egg yolk. Sift together the flour and salt into the mixture and stir until combined. Halve the dough, form it into two balls, wrap in clingfilm and chill in the refrigerator for 30–60 minutes.

Preheat the oven to 190°C/375°F/Gas Mark 5. Line two large baking sheets with greaseproof paper. Roll out the dough between two sheets of greaseproof paper. Cut out rounds with a 6-cm/2½-inch cutter and place them on the baking sheets, spaced well apart. Bake in the preheated oven for 10–12 minutes, or until golden brown. Leave to cool on the baking sheets for 5 minutes, then transfer to wire racks to cool completely.

To make the icing, sift the icing sugar into a bowl, add the lemon extract and stir in the hot water to achieve a smooth consistency. Spread over the cookies and leave to set.

White Chocolate Cakes

makes 18

115 g/4 oz butter, softened, plus extra for greasing

85 g/3 oz sugar

2 eggs, lightly beaten

150 g/5½ oz self-raising flour

2 tbsp milk

85 g/3 oz plain chocolate chips

25 g/1 oz cocoa powder

For the icing

140 g/5 oz white chocolate

175 g/6 oz low-fat soft cheese

Preheat the oven to 180°C/350°F/Gas Mark 4. Lightly grease 18 holes in two muffin tins.

Beat together the butter and sugar until pale and fluffy. Gradually add the eggs, beating well after each addition. Add a little of the flour if the mixture begins to curdle. Stir in the milk, then fold in the chocolate chips.

Sift together the remaining flour and cocoa powder and fold into the mixture with a metal spoon. Divide the mixture equally between the muffin holes and level the tops.

Bake in the preheated oven for 20 minutes or until well risen and springy to the touch. Leave to cool on a wire rack.

To make the icing, put the chocolate in a heatproof bowl set over a saucepan of gently simmering water and heat until melted. Allow to cool slightly. Beat the soft cheese until softened slightly, then beat in the melted chocolate. Spread the icing over each cake and chill in the refrigerator for 1 hour before serving.

Cinnamon Swirl Bundt Cake

serves 6-8

280 g/10 oz plain flour, plus extra for dusting

1 tsp baking powder

1 tsp bicarbonate of soda

½ tsp salt

175 g/6 oz unsalted butter, plus extra for greasing

300 g/10½ oz caster sugar

3 large eggs

225 g/8 oz soured cream

1 tsp vanilla extract

55 g/2 oz walnuts, chopped (optional)

For the swirl

1 tbsp ground cinnamon

3 tbsp muscovado sugar

2 tbsp granulated sugar

For the glaze

125 g/4½ oz icing sugar

1½ tbsp milk

1 tsp ground cinnamon, or to taste

Preheat the oven to 180°C/350°F/Gas Mark 4. Grease a 25-cm/10-inch bundt tin and lightly dust with flour.

Whisk together the flour, baking powder, bicarbonate of soda and salt in a mixing bowl for 1 minute and reserve until needed.

Cream the butter and sugar together until light and fluffy. Beat in the eggs one at a time, mixing thoroughly before adding the next. Beat in the soured cream and vanilla extract until combined. Add the flour mixture, stirring just until combined. Stir in the walnuts, if using.

Pour half the batter into the prepared tin and spread evenly. Mix all the ingredients for the swirl in a small bowl. Sprinkle evenly around the centre of the cake mix in the tin. Cover with the rest of the batter.

Bake in the preheated oven for 50 minutes or until a skewer inserted in the centre comes out clean. Leave to cool for 20 minutes before removing from the tin.

For the glaze, put the icing sugar in a small mixing bowl and stir in enough milk to create a thick but pourable glaze. Stir in the cinnamon to taste. Drizzle over the top of the cake. Once the icing is set, slice and serve.

Apple & Cinnamon Bars

For the base

125 g/4½ oz unsalted butter, plus extra for greasing

125 g/4½ oz golden caster sugar

1 tsp vanilla extract

2 eggs, beaten

150 g/5½ oz self-raising flour

2 large eating apples

2 tbsp lemon juice

For the topping

40 g/1½ oz blanched almonds, finely chopped

40 g/1½ oz plain flour

40 g/1½ oz light muscovado sugar

½ tsp ground cinnamon

30 g/1 oz unsalted butter, melted

Preheat the oven to 180°C/350°F/Gas Mark 4. Grease and line a 28 x 18-cm/11 x 7-inch rectangular baking tin.

Cream together the butter, sugar and vanilla extract until pale. Gradually add the eggs, beating thoroughly. Sift in the flour and fold in evenly.

Prepare the apples by peeling, dicing and sprinkling with the lemon juice. Add to the flour mixture and stir to combine.

Spread the mixture over the base of the baking tin. Even out with the back of a wooden spoon or palette knife.

For the topping, mix together all the ingredients to a crumbly texture and sprinkle over the base. Bake in the preheated oven for 45–55 minutes until firm and golden.

Cut into bars and serve warm or cooled.

Loaf Cake with Orange Glaze

serves 6-8

25 g/1 oz butter, for greasing

250 g/9 oz plain flour, plus extra for dusting

1 tsp baking powder

¼ tsp bicarbonate of soda

½ tsp salt

225 g/8 oz unsalted butter

250 g/9 oz caster sugar

1 tbsp grated lemon zest

1 tbsp grated orange zest

4 eggs

125 ml/4 fl oz buttermilk

For the glaze

125 g/4½ oz icing sugar

1 tbsp freshly grated orange zest

1½ tbsp fresh orange juice, or as needed

Preheat the oven to 160°C/325°F/Gas Mark 3. Grease a 450-g/1-lb loaf tin and dust with flour. Set aside.

Sift together the flour, baking powder, bicarbonate of soda and salt in a mixing bowl. Set aside.

In another mixing bowl, use an electric whisk to beat the butter, sugar and zests until very light and creamy. Beat in the eggs one at time, mixing very thoroughly between each addition. Mix in the flour mixture and buttermilk alternating between each and ending with an addition of flour. Scrape the mixture into the prepared loaf tin.

Bake in the preheated oven for 1 hour–1¼ hours, or until a skewer inserted in the centre comes out clean. Remove and leave to rest for 15 minutes, then transfer to a wire rack. Leave to cool for a further 15 minutes before glazing.

Combine the orange glaze ingredients in a bowl, adding enough orange juice to achieve a smooth spreadable consistency. Apply to the top of the warm cake. Allow the cake to cool completely before slicing.

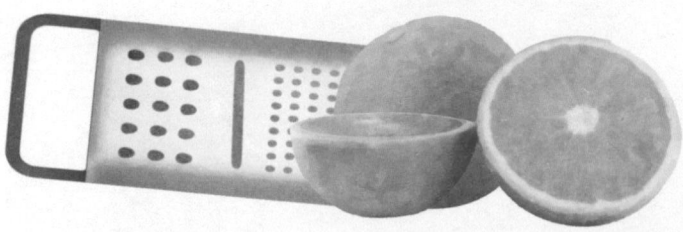

Fruit Crumble Tart

For the pastry
150 g/5½ oz plain flour, plus extra for dusting

2 tbsp caster sugar

115 g/4 oz butter, diced

1 tbsp water

For the filling
175 g/6 oz raspberries

350 g/12 oz plums, halved, stoned and roughly chopped

3 tbsp muscovado sugar

For the topping
125 g/4½ oz plain flour

85 g/3 oz muscovado sugar

55 g/2 oz butter, diced

85 g/3 oz mixed nuts, chopped

1 tsp ground cinnamon

Cream or custard, to serve

Preheat the oven to 200°C/400°F/Gas Mark 6.

To make the pastry, place the flour, sugar and butter in a bowl and rub in the butter with your fingertips. Add the water and bring together with your fingers to form a soft dough. Wrap in clingfilm and chill in the refrigerator for 30 minutes.

Roll out the pastry on a lightly floured work surface and use it to line the base of a deep 23-cm/9-inch loose-based flan tin. Prick the base of the tart case with a fork and chill in the refrigerator for about 30 minutes.

To make the filling, toss the raspberries and plums together with the sugar and spoon into the tart case.

To make the crumble topping, combine the flour, sugar and butter in a bowl. Rub in the butter with your fingertips until the mixture resembles coarse breadcrumbs. Stir in the nuts and ground cinnamon.

Sprinkle the crumble topping over the fruit and press down gently with the back of a spoon. Bake in the preheated oven for 20–25 minutes until the topping has turned golden brown. Serve with cream or custard.

Chocolate & Apricot Squares

makes 9

115 g/4 oz butter, plus extra for greasing

125 g/4½ oz white chocolate, broken into pieces

4 eggs

100 g/3½ oz caster sugar

280 g/10 oz plain flour

1 tsp baking powder

Pinch of salt

70 g/2½ oz ready-to-eat dried apricots, chopped

Preheat the oven to 180°C/350°F/Gas Mark 4.

Lightly grease a 23-cm/9-inch square cake tin and line the base with baking paper.

Melt the butter and chocolate in a heatproof bowl set over a saucepan of simmering water. Stir frequently with a wooden spoon until the mixture is smooth and glossy. Remove from the heat and leave the chocolate mixture to cool slightly.

Beat the eggs and sugar into the butter and chocolate mixture until well combined. In a large bowl, sift together the flour, baking powder and salt and add the apricots. Add the chocolate batter and mix together well.

Pour the mixture into the prepared tin and bake in the preheated oven for 25–30 minutes.

The centre of the cake may not be completely firm when you take it out of the oven, but it will set as it cools. Leave it to cool in the tin.

When the cake is completely cold, turn it out of the tin and carefully slice into squares to serve.

Black & White Brownies

makes 24

115 g/4 oz butter

350 g/12 oz plain chocolate, broken into pieces

For the cream cheese mix

85 g/3 oz butter

225 g/8 oz soft cheese

150 g/5½ oz caster sugar

3 eggs

3 tbsp flour

1 tbsp vanilla extract

For the chocolate mix

6 eggs

450 g/1 lb caster sugar

150 g/5½ oz plain flour

1½ tsp baking powder

1½ tsp salt

1½ tbsp vanilla extract

1 tsp almond extract

Preheat the oven to 180°C/350°F/Gas Mark 4. Line a 33 x 23-cm/13 x 9-inch baking tin with baking paper.

Slowly melt the butter and the chocolate in a heatproof bowl set over a saucepan of gently simmering water until melted. Mix well and set aside to cool.

For the cream cheese mix, cream the butter with an electric whisk, then add the soft cheese and sugar, and beat until fluffy. Add the eggs, then the flour and the vanilla extract.

Make the chocolate mix in a separate bowl. Whip the eggs and sugar until fluffy. In another bowl, stir together the flour, baking powder and salt, then mix into the egg mixture. Finally, mix in the melted chocolate and butter, the vanilla and almond extract.

Spread half the chocolate mixture in the prepared tin and spread the cream cheese layer over the top of the chocolate mixture. Spoon the remaining chocolate mixture on the top. Swirl with a knife to create a marbled effect. Bake in the preheated oven for 40 minutes. Cool completely, then cut into bars.

Chocolate & Walnut Cake with Icing

serves 6-8

25 g/1 oz butter, melted, plus extra for greasing

4 eggs

100 g/3½ oz caster sugar

125 g/4½ oz plain flour

1 tbsp cocoa powder

55 g/2 oz plain chocolate, broken into pieces, melted

150 g/5½ oz walnuts, finely chopped

For the icing

55 g/2 oz plain chocolate, broken into pieces

115 g/4 oz butter

150 g/5½ oz icing sugar

2 tbsp milk

Walnut halves, for decorating

Preheat the oven to 160°C/325°F/Gas Mark 3. Grease a 15-cm/6-inch round cake tin with butter and line with greaseproof paper.

Place the eggs and sugar in a mixing bowl and whisk with an electric whisk for 10 minutes, or until the mixture is light and foamy and the whisk leaves a trail that lasts a few seconds when lifted.

Sift together the flour and cocoa powder into a separate bowl and fold into the eggs and sugar with a metal spoon. Fold in the melted butter, chocolate and the chopped walnuts.

Pour the mixture into the prepared tin and bake in the preheated oven for 30–35 minutes, or until springy to the touch. Leave to cool in the tin for 5 minutes, then transfer to a wire rack to cool completely. Cut the cold cake into two layers.

To make the icing, melt the chocolate in a heatproof bowl set over a saucepan of gently simmering water and heat until melted. Leave to cool slightly. Beat together the butter, icing sugar and milk in a bowl until the mixture is pale and fluffy. Whisk in the melted chocolate.

Sandwich the two cake layers with some of the icing and place on a serving plate. Spread the remaining icing over the top of the cake with a palette knife, swirling it slightly as you go. Decorate with the walnut halves and serve.

Fruit Loaf

serves 8

Corn oil, for brushing
175 g/6 oz porridge oats
100 g/3½ oz muscovado sugar
1 tsp ground cinnamon
115 g/4 oz sultanas
150 g/5½ oz seedless raisins
2 tbsp malt extract
300 ml/10 fl oz apple juice
125 g/4½ oz self-raising wholemeal flour
1½ tsp baking powder

Preheat the oven to 180°C/350°F/Gas Mark 4. Grease a 900-g/2-lb loaf tin and line with greaseproof paper.

Place the oats, sugar, cinnamon, sultanas, raisins and malt extract in a bowl. Pour in the apple juice, stir well and leave to soak for 30 minutes.

Sift the flour and baking powder into the mixture.

Spoon the mixture into the prepared tin and bake in the preheated oven for 1½ hours, or until firm and a skewer inserted in the centre comes out clean.

Leave to cool in the tin for 10 minutes, then turn out onto a wire rack to cool completely.

Index

almonds
    Almond Biscuits 181
    Apple & Cinnamon Bars 207
apples
    Apple & Cinnamon Bars 207
    Blackberry & Apple Cake 180
    Chicken & Apple Bake 142
    Rich Apple Scones 195
    Spiced Apple Ring 190
apricots
    Chocolate & Apricot Squares 211
artichokes
    Hot Spinach & Artichoke Dip 41
    Pan-cooked Chicken 155
aubergines
    Pork Chops & Spicy Beans 99
    Vegetable Lasagne 100
    Vegetable Soup with Cannellini Beans 63
avocados
    Chicken, Bacon & Avocado Salad 74
    Potato Skins with Guacamole 66

bacon
    Bacon & Lentil Soup 55
    Baked Spinach & Feta Omelette 24
    Braised Thin Ribs of Beef 158
    Chicken, Bacon & Avocado Salad 74
    Clam Chowder 64
    Eggs Benedict 14
    Fried Chicken with Tomato & Bacon Sauce 97
    Pasta with Bacon & Tomatoes 122
    Pot Roast Lamb 163
    Spaghetti Bolognese 104
beans
    Chilli con Carne 129
    Jacket Potatoes with Beans 78
    Minestrone Soup 58
    Pork Chops & Spicy Beans 99
    Refried Beans with Tortillas 51
    Sausage & Beans 94
    Vegetable Soup with Cannellini Beans 63
beef
    Beef & Vegetable Stew with Corn Cobs 161
    Beef Soup with Rice 46

Braised Thin Ribs of Beef 158
Chilli con Carne 129
Classic Beef Fajitas 93
Corned Beef Hash 20
Fried Steak with White Gravy 169
Grandma's Meatloaf 88
Meatballs with Tomato Relish 112
Pot Roast Beef 146
Spaghetti & Meatballs 134
Spaghetti Bolognese 104
Steak Mince in Tomato Sauce on a Bap 117
Steak Topped with Mushrooms 110
Wing Rib of Beef 132
see also salt beef
beetroot
    Meatballs with Tomato Relish 112
biscuits & cookies
    Almond Biscuits 181
    Chequerboard Biscuits 198
    Chocolate Chip Biscuits 187
    Lemon & Sesame Seed Cookies 202
    Peanut Butter Cookies 193
black-eyed beans
    Chicken with Black-eyed Beans 105
    Jacket Potatoes with Beans 78
blackberries
    Blackberry & Apple Cake 180
    Cheesecake with Fruit Sauce 186
bread
    Baked Herb Ricotta 43
    Eggy French Bread 21
    Tomato & Cheese Bruschetta 75
broccoli
    Chinese Chicken & Rice 162
    Turkey with Orange & Rice 91
buttermilk
    Buttermilk Fried Chicken 151
    Buttermilk Scones 31
    Chocolate Marshmallow Cake 199
    Loaf Cake with Orange Glaze 208
    Smothered Pork Chops 152

cabbage
    Minestrone Soup 58
    Salt Beef & Cabbage 120

ham
    Gammon Cooked in Cider 103
    Minestrone Soup 58
    Stuffed Pork with Prosciutto 149
horseradish
    Devilled Eggs 40
    Prawn Cocktail 72

lamb
    Braised Lamb Shanks 138
    Pot Roast Lamb 163
leeks
    Chicken & Autumn Vegetable Bake 166
    Layered Vegetable Bake 125
    Potato, Leek & Chicken Pie 123
    Stuffed Mushrooms 67
    Vegetable Cake 70
    Vegetable Soup with Cannellini
      Beans 63
lemons
    Lemon & Sesame Seed Cookies 202
    Lemon Poppy Seed Muffins 22
lentils
    Bacon & Lentil Soup 55
    Turkey & Lentil Soup 80
limes
    Baked Fish with Lime 98
    Chicken with Lime Stuffing 113
    Classic Beef Fajitas 93

muffins
    Banana Cinnamon Muffins 17
    Chocolate Chip Muffins 27
    Lemon Poppy Seed Muffins 22
mushrooms
    Chicken & Autumn Vegetable Bake 166
    Chinese Chicken & Rice 162
    Grandma's Meatloaf 88
    Macaroni & Tuna Layer 92
    Potato, Leek & Chicken Pie 123
    Prawns with Coconut Rice 114
    Rösti with Tomato Sauce 82
    Sausage & Mushroom Breakfast Frittata 28
    Steak Topped with Mushrooms 110
    Stuffed Mushrooms 67
    Stuffed Tomatoes 47
    Turkey & Lentil Soup 80
    Vegetable Lasagne 100
    Vegetable Soup with Cannellini Beans 63

nuts
    Carrot Cake with Cream Cheese Icing 188
    Chocolate & Walnut Cake with Icing 214

Chocolate Chip Biscuits 187
Fruit Crumble Tart 210
Peanut Butter Cookies 193
Spiced Apple Ring 190

see also almonds; pecan nuts; walnuts

oats
    Flapjacks 177
    Fruit Loaf 215
okra
    Chicken & Sausage Gumbo 148
olives
    Niçoise Pasta Salad 79
    Stuffed Garlic Chicken 159
    Stuffed Pork with Prosciutto 149
    Tomato & Cheese Bruschetta 75
    Turkey with Orange & Rice 91
omelettes
    Baked Spinach & Feta Omelette 24
    Spanish Potato Omelette 16
oranges
    Beef Soup with Rice 46
    Chocolate & Orange Ring 176
    Loaf Cake with Orange Glaze 208
    Turkey with Orange & Rice 91

pancakes
    Blueberry Pancakes 34
    Potato Pancakes with Smoked Salmon & Dill
      Crème Fraîche 19
parsnips
    Chicken & Autumn Vegetable Bake 166
    Pot Roast Beef 146
pasta & noodles
    Chicken & Pasta Broth 69
    Creamy Pasta with Peas 141
    Macaroni & Tuna Layer 92
    Minestrone Soup 58
    Niçoise Pasta Salad 79
    Pasta with Bacon & Tomatoes 122
    Pork & Vegetable Soup 77
    Spaghetti & Meatballs 134
    Spaghetti Bolognese 104
    Spicy Tomato Tagliatelle 154
    Vegetable Lasagne 100
    Vegetable Soup with Cannellini Beans 63
peas
    Beef & Vegetable Stew with Corn Cobs 161
    Creamy Pasta with Peas 141
    Minestrone Soup 58
    Rösti with Tomato Sauce 82
    Spicy Pork & Rice 140

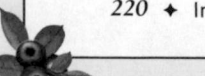

Happy Cooking from Blueberry Hill